Photograph copyright Russell Booth

In this book Gail Gifford reflects on extraordinary experiences encountered while working as a teacher in Zambia, Nigeria, and Malaysia. Influenced by these incredible demonstrations of the power of mind over body, and excited by the possibilities of using this for therapy and healing, Gail went on to study with renowned international psychotherapists. She then opened her own successful hypnotherapy practice and ran hypnotherapy training courses for many years. Gail also worked as a Senior Psychological Therapist for the National Health Service in the UK. Now retired, she lives with her family on an island off the east coast of Australia.

Disclaimer

The information in this book relates to various conditions and treatment of clients who came to me for hypnotherapy.

The information in this book is not intended to be a substitute for professional medical advice or treatment.

Names and places have been removed and some details have been altered to protect and respect the identity of the client. Any resemblance to any persons living or dead is coincidental.

The stories, however, are true.

The Man Who Screamed with Seagulls

Gail Gifford

The Man Who Screamed with Seagulls

Vanguard Press

VANGUARD PAPERBACK

© Copyright 2024
Gail Gifford

The right of Gail Gifford to be identified as author of
this work has been asserted by her in accordance with the
Copyright, Designs and Patents Act 1988.

All Rights Reserved

No reproduction, copy or transmission of this publication
may be made without written permission.
No paragraph of this publication may be reproduced,
copied or transmitted save with the written permission of the publisher, or in
accordance with the provisions
of the Copyright Act 1956 (as amended).

Any person who commits any unauthorised act in relation to
this publication may be liable to criminal
prosecution and civil claims for damages.

A CIP catalogue record for this title is
available from the British Library.

ISBN 978 1 83794 097 4

*Vanguard Press is an imprint of
Pegasus Elliot Mackenzie Publishers Ltd.*
www.pegasuspublishers.com

First Published in 2024

**Vanguard Press
Sheraton House Castle Park
Cambridge England**

Printed & Bound in Great Britain

This book is dedicated to:

My sister Val, who has always been there for me.
My Australian family
Anna, Russell, Emma and Imogen.
Dr Clare Jefferson
a talented clinician and cherished friend.
and
Norman Vaughton
a valued mentor and true gentleman.

FOREWORD

by Clare Jefferson

I had the good fortune of meeting Gail at the beginning of my career when I was fresh out of university and eager to help people with the ideas and approaches I had discovered. I knew psychology had the potential to change lives but of course I had no idea about what that looked like, or what it meant to genuinely sit alongside someone during their most vulnerable moments.

Gail was my first mentor, and I was simply dazzled by and in awe of her work in equal measure. This amazing woman so kindly welcomed me into the world of psychology and generously shared her wisdom with me. I barely understood a word she said! Nonetheless, she patiently guided me through those naïve years and fundamentally shaped me into the clinician I am today. There are many things Gail has taught me about therapy and life, including the fundamental importance of trusting that the story will unfold in its own time, listening well to the struggles a person can describe and believing that the experiences recounted makes sense, even if we cannot logically understand why. Gail also helped me to find the courage early on to sit with the struggle and story as it unfolded and 'fly by the seat of my pants' with every new client I met. Consistently, these qualities are what clients have appreciated most when we have reflected back on the therapy journey together.

As therapists, we are constantly humbled and surprised by the willingness of people to share their story with us so that we can walk alongside them for a little while during their change journey. This book honours the people Gail has been privileged to meet and the stories that they have courageously shared with her. This book came into being because many of the clients Gail has met have touched her heart in some way and she has carried them and their experiences along with her. It chronicles the appreciation and respect Gail has for those who have suffered and found their way to the safe haven of her clinic room. It is born from the empathic connection she has with people and journals her personal reflections on the wounds people are left with when others are cruel. It also details the incredible changes she has witnessed from her unique and exceptional application of hypnotherapy.

Throughout the wonderful chapters you are about to read, you will connect with human struggles and pain, examples of what people take away from therapy, and the profound changes that have been made to lives after spending time with Gail. It's impossible to read this book without being moved to tears, chuckling at the humour throughout, or being awestruck by the resilience and capacity that people have to heal. People take from therapy what they need at that moment in time, and this is an invitation for you to do just that. As you read on there will be stories that resonate powerfully with you and others that may be more difficult to understand and relate to. This is absolutely as it should be. Just take what you need from the book.

Gail is my mentor and my closest friend. To spend time in her company is restorative and transformative. Given that you have found this book, I assume that you are interested in what it is to be human and understand suffering and struggling too. Therefore, my wish is that you find hope and comfort in these pages as you connect with the lived experiences of others and the impact of therapy with a real person who fundamentally understands what people need.

If you make the decision to try therapy for yourself, please check that the therapist is an accredited practitioner, their professional registration status, their clinical supervision arrangements, and obtain feedback from other clients before you meet with them. Hopefully you will sense the importance of meeting with a therapist who is captivated by their field and as dedicated in their quest to learn more, in the way that Gail has been. She was so determined to understand hypnotherapy and help people with it that not only did she dedicate years to learning, she also taught many other practitioners' hypnotherapy so that they could also skilfully and safely help the clients they worked with.

I close where I began. I have been fortunate to know Gail for over twenty years. She continues to guide me from afar and I know I would not be the clinician I am today without her in my life.

Thank you, Gail.

Dr Clare Jefferson.
Consultant Clinical Psychologist and Clinical Lead.

FOREWORD

by Norman Vaughton

I have known Gail and had the privilege of working with her both as her tutor and subsequently as her colleague at The Academy of Curative Hypnotherapists.

Over the years, Gail studied with many eminent international hypnotherapists, acquiring several different techniques and skills to use at her command. These she utilised in a wonderfully eclectic way, guided by an instinctive wisdom that I am sure is utterly innate in her. Gail was not limited to following rigid procedures or sticking to one school of practice. Gathering information from a client with apparently innocent and simple questions, she responded often with uniquely devised approaches that perfectly suited their needs and idiosyncrasies.

This volume of tales perfectly illustrates the magic Gail commanded in her therapeutic practice and the unique genius, creativity, and flexibility she had in her work. It is extremely readable and is written with great modesty – one can only wonder at the great good fortune of those encountering her as their therapist. I trust you will read these case histories with the same delight and wonder they afforded me!

Norman Vaughton B.SC, A.K.C, Dip.Ed, F.R.G.S, D.H.C, C.R.C, F.A.C.H.

Throughout this book, to clarify when I am talking directly to the unconscious mind of a client in trance, my words are written in *italics*.

The words I use are simple, the phrases and sentences are short and uncomplicated, often acknowledging and repeating the client's last response, so that they are aware that they have been really heard. I use 'Clean Language' learnt from David Grove, which reduces the influence of the therapist on the client. It is in the client's memory that the reasons or causes for the presenting problems or symptom can be discovered and where often the solution can be found. Using carefully considered questions that interfere with the client's therapeutic experience the least, is most effective in bringing about positive and permanent change.

'There are more things in heaven and earth, Horatio,
Than are dreamt of in your philosophy.'

From Hamlet (1.5.167 – 168).
Hamlet to Horatio
by William Shakespeare.

Contents

FOREWORD by Clare Jefferson	9
FOREWORD by Norman Vaughton	13
INTRODUCTION	21
THE MAN WHO CRIED	36
I HATE TUESDAYS	43
SMOKING IS MY ONLY COMFORT	50
WARTS AND ALL	56
TO HAVE AND HAVE NOT	65
THE SECRET OF HAPPINESS	72
THAT'S CLASSIFIED	79
PREVENT THE EVENT	87
THE MAN WITH THE CLAW	92
UNABLE TO LET GO	101
THE MAN WHO SCREAMED WITH SEAGULLS	110
A FREE LUNCH	124
PLEASE LEAVE YOUR NAME AND NUMBER	128
GROUNDED BY FEAR	133
THAT SINKING FEELING	141
MADAM MY WILLY IS NOT WORKING WELL	149
THE POWER OF LOVE	157
MORE THAN WORDS CAN SAY	165
SCARED TO DEATH	177
DOWN CAME A BLACKBIRD	188
FOOD FOR THOUGHT	197
STARVED OF AFFECTION – HUNGRY FOR LOVE	208
GIVING TALKS – MEMORABLE FOR THE WRONG REASONS!	215
AFTERWORD	224
Acknowledgements	228

INTRODUCTION

I never set out to be a hypnotherapist.

I trained as a teacher. In 1966 my husband and I as newly qualified teachers went to work in Zambia at Senanga Secondary School in Barotse Province, situated on the banks of the mighty Zambezi River. There were a lot of surprises, including the ages of the students, some of whom were in their forties. Over a thousand students arrived at the Boarding School on the first day. Most had grown up living in mud huts in remote villages, but fortunately, nearly all spoke basic English, which they had learnt at mission schools. Everyone had a lot of adjustments to make, and I realised early on that the training I'd received in England was not going to address the many challenges I now faced in Zambia.

During the day, the air was so hot it hurt to inhale, and flies covered my face and body when I stepped outside. Everyone existed in a cloud of flies, we ate, spoke, and breathed flies and soon learned to ignore them. We were provided with basic accommodation in the grounds of the school. At night it was difficult to sleep with the heat and the constant sound of drumming from the surrounding villages, which would continue well into the evening. Our bed was enclosed under fine white netting, suspended from hooks in the ceiling. I found this extremely claustrophobic, but it was necessary to prevent us from getting malaria from the swarms of mosquitoes that whined against the material that shrouded our bed. For several weeks of the year, we were deafened by the shrill vibration of millions of cicadas that emerged after years spent deep underground. These large black and green grasshopper-like insects were welcomed as a tasty treat by the locals, who would collect and roast them over open fires, eating them salted and crunchy as we would eat nuts.

I became pregnant and continued to teach right up to my due date. In Zambia at that time, women were considered to be of little consequence, with less value than that of a cow, and as a pregnant female, I did not have much status in the eyes of many of the older male students.

Zambia gained independence from British Colonial rule in 1964 under the leadership of Kenneth Kaunda. Kaunda's father and (unusually for the time), his mother had both been teachers. Consequently, he had been well educated. He trained as a teacher before embarking on the political path, which would eventually see him become elected as the first President of the newly independent Zambia – a position he kept until 1991, despite several coup attempts.

As a former teacher, Kaunda was aware of the importance of education. When he became President he promised free, quality schooling for all Zambians, instituting a policy where each child would be provided with free exercise books, pens, and pencils. This policy led to a huge demand for qualified teachers, which is why my husband and I were in Zambia. Parents who had previously been unable to afford to send their children to school were eager to have their children benefit from this free education. I found myself in the bizarre situation of teaching classes in which married men, who had missed out on completing their education, now returned to school. They wore uniforms many sizes too small for them, as they sat uncomfortably hunched at the small wooden desks built for children.

I had been working at the school for a few months when the staff were informed, with great excitement by the headmaster, that President Kaunda was visiting. He would honour us by flying in with his ministers to see the progress made at our new school. I was on duty the day before he was due to arrive and was given the task of assembling all the students to rehearse, singing the new National Anthem – which had replaced 'God Save the Queen.' Entitled 'Stand and Sing of Zambia, Proud and Free,' it was thankfully in English.

There were no other members of staff present as the students were released from their classrooms, and they filed out reluctantly into the dusty courtyard to stand under the blazing midday sun. I was single-handedly attempting to line up one thousand students, with the eldest boys at the front (because they were deemed to be more important), followed by the eldest girls and younger students towards the back. The students were not happy, and neither was I – standing there, nine months pregnant, hot, sweaty, covered in flies totally overwhelmed by the magnitude of the task.

In the front row, a mature male student refused to line up in the position I had indicated. He was extremely rude and confrontational, and it soon became apparent that he objected to being told where to stand by a woman. In exasperation, I told him off loudly, indicating again where he should stand. There was a collective gasp from the other students and then silence as they stood and stared. The male student raised his arm, pointed directly at me, and started chanting loudly and rolling his eyes – I was astonished. Pandemonium ensued as students reacted by screaming and crying, running frantically away from me, past the buildings and disappearing into the surrounding bush. I was left alone with the student, who finished chanting and coughed up a ball of phlegm which he spat with great precision at my feet before turning and walking away. I was unsure what had just happened, but I knew it wasn't good. Other staff came rushing out into the courtyard, demanding to know what I had done! I had no students, and we still had not practised lining up or singing the National Anthem. It was a disaster.

The next morning, I arrived early at school, hoping to salvage the situation by assembling the students to practise the anthem before the President arrived. I was surprised to find the school deserted. The students were nowhere to be seen. I walked over to the senior girl's dormitories, which were simple huts set up like army barracks with beds on either side. As I entered a building, the girls started screaming when they saw me. Some fainted while others ran away, and a few even jumped out of the windows. I managed to corner one girl who was shaking with fear, unable to look me in the eye. I spoke gently to her and asked her what was going on. It took a long time for her to explain that the male student I had reprimanded the previous day was known to be a powerful witch doctor, and he had put a death curse on me. Apparently, the curse meant that I should have died that night. All the students looking at me now believed that I was dead and had been in terror when they saw me, as they thought I was a vengeful walking ghost!

I assured the girl that I had not died and was not a ghost. I held out my arm and made her touch me to prove I was warm and alive. She calmed down and called to the other girls, who were watching nervously from outside the windows. They finally came in, got dressed in their uniforms and walked back with me into the school courtyard. When the boys saw the girls returning, they didn't want to be humiliated by being considered less brave than the girls, so they also slowly started to assemble in the courtyard.

Finally, with help from other staff members, I got all the students lined up, and we practised the national anthem without incident – just in time as the cavalcade of dust-covered Land Rovers brought our very important visitors from the airstrip. As the dignitaries sat down, switching their fly swats made from wildebeest tails, the school staff stood respectfully to one side. President Kaunda waved his trademark white handkerchief for attention, leaned over, spoke to the headmaster, and asked for a chair for the pregnant teacher. A chair was brought, and I sat down gratefully. All went well, and the students stood and sang the national anthem enthusiastically. Speeches were made, the school was inspected, refreshments were enjoyed, and then the dignitaries returned to the Land Rovers and left in another cloud of dust. I was exhausted.

A few days later, I went into labour. I was driven by my husband over dirt roads to the only medical facility in the area, a small hospital that had been built many years earlier by Dr Cassalis. She was a resourceful Swiss missionary who had travelled along the Zambezi River, transported in a dugout canoe, braving the crocodiles and hippos to establish the hospital which provided much-needed treatment for people afflicted with leprosy.

The hospital was very basic, it had no electricity or running water, and the only pain relief available was a mask with liquid ether dripped onto the gauze. My daughter Anna was born later that night by the light of a hissing kerosene lamp in a thatched rondavel hut with a beaten earth and cow-dung floor. My husband, esteemed in the community for his bravery and prowess at hunting, was so overwhelmed by the horror of the birth that he fainted and had to be carried from the hut.

Male and female leprosy patients who had lost noses, ears, fingers, and toes to the terrible disease were unable to return to their villages. They now lived in a separate compound attached to the hospital. When the women heard that I was in labour, they came to support me in childbirth and watched the proceedings with interest through the glassless windows and door, singing aloud with joy when my baby finally emerged. The baby book I had brought with me from England had certainly not prepared me for any of this!

I spoke to Dr Cassalis about my experience with the witch doctor, and she warned me to be very careful, as he would have lost face by my failure to die. She thought he might try to kill me by other means to assert the potency of his curse. I heeded her warning and we slept with a rifle by the bed and our dogs loose inside the house. Five days later, my precious baby was wrapped in a cloth and tied to a village girl's back, as was the local custom, and I resumed teaching full-time. I would return home mid-morning each day from school to breastfeed my baby. Outside the door on the steps of the house, I would often find gifts of wooden animal carvings, fresh vegetables, fruit, fish, and live hobbled chickens. They were from people I didn't even know who wanted to welcome the safe delivery of my baby into the community, for which I was deeply touched.

The experience of being cursed by the witch doctor and witnessing firsthand the reaction of the students who believed I must be dead, was the first time I truly understood the absolute power of belief and suggestion. I came to understand over time that people from different backgrounds had diffcrent ideas of normal, different beliefs and different expectations. In Africa, my mind was opened to many things that I would not have experienced, considered or even known about had I remained in England. In hindsight, I believe that each new experience helped me to see things from a different perspective and would, in time, have a positive effect on the way I interacted with clients as a therapist.

Interestingly, following the witch doctor incident and the president's courtesy, I was then treated with the greatest respect by all students and the Zambian staff. It was generally perceived that because neither I nor my unborn baby had died from the curse, I must be in possession of a magic that was even stronger and more powerful than the witch doctor. He did not return to the school, and I was later told that he had moved away from the area, fortunately, we never saw him again.

Two years later, I chose to return to England for the birth of my second child. We selected a private nursing home near my parents, and I hoped for luxury, running water, electricity, and pain relief after the traumatic experience at the leprosy hospital. However, after being subjected to the strict rules and regimes of the overbearing Catholic Nuns who dictated when I could wash, eat, sleep or change, hold and feed my baby, I found myself longing for the simplicity and freedom of the mud hut and the kindness of strangers that had surrounded me. After two days, I couldn't stand it anymore and ran away from the nursing home, picking up my son Roger and checking out early, despite having paid for a ten-day stay.

After two years of living in England, we returned to Africa, settling in Nigeria this time, where I taught in Maiduguri in the Northeast State as Head of Education in a Teacher Training College. In 1974 our family moved again, this time to the west coast of Malaysia, where I set up and was Head Teacher of an International School in Melaka.

My sister, Val, visited me in Malaysia for a holiday. I had not seen her for over two years since the birth of my son. When she stepped off the plane in Kuala Lumpur, I hardly recognised her because she was so slim. When I'd last seen her, she had been very overweight. I was delighted for her and asked how this had happened.

"Hypnosis!" she told me.

It was wonderful having my sister to stay, and we made the most of our time visiting temples, mosques, and antique shops. We went to a cobbler who gave her a tiny, embroidered lotus shoe that had been worn by an old Chinese lady whose feet had been broken and bound as a child. Val had dresses made for her new slim body by a skilled local tailor, who measured her one day and had all her clothes perfectly finished by the next. We swam, barbecued, and took boat trips over to the island of Pulau Besar. We enjoyed wonderful meals at Chinese, Portuguese and Indian Restaurants and browsed stalls at night markets along the Melaka River. We were told of a religious ceremony at a local temple where there was going to be firewalking, and we decided to go.

We arrived in the heat of the day and followed the crowd down to the river. It was dusty and noisy, with beating of drums and blowing of instruments. Coloured powders were flung into the air, and the scent of jasmine garlands, sandalwood and incense was overpowering. After ritually bathing in the river, a hundred or so devotees lined up to have a metal pole skewered through one cheek and out of the other. They didn't react to the piercing, as they were already deeply in trance. Some had smaller trident-ended metal poles inserted through their protruding tongues. Some had their backs pierced with huge metal hooks, and some were attached by cords from these hooks to ornate-coloured temples that they carried balanced on their head and shoulders. The hooks strained at their skin, pulling it into tented peaks from the weight they supported. The believers had ash daubed on their foreheads, their eyes were intense but unfocused, and they made no sound as they joined the procession, the crowd parting to let them through.

The constant rhythmic music was overpowering. I looked around for Val to find she was caught up in the moment. She had moved closer to where the devotees were being pierced and was watching the process in fascination, but I couldn't watch the poles and hooks being inserted – I told myself it was her medical background that made the difference! I worked my way through the crowd towards her and pulled her away, Val was swaying to the music, and her eyes were glazed over. I became concerned for her well-being and suggested we leave and go home. However, she wanted to stay to witness the fire walking that we had come to see. By this time, Val had also made friends with an elderly Indian man who kindly took it upon himself to explain to us both what was happening. He supervised my sister in taking acceptable photographs of the ceremony, ensuring that she was not being invasive and that no one was offended.

The procession moved slowly onto the road heading towards the temple, and once again, we were swept along with the crowd.

Rickshaws passed, the riders ringing their bells, cars drove by with drivers sounding their horns, but no one paid any attention to the traffic.

Finally, we reached the temple, where our guide informed us that the long fire pit had been burning since early that morning. It was now white-hot ash that had been raked into a long low mound about eight metres in length and about two metres wide. Standing close to the fire was impossible as the heat was unbearable. The air above shimmered and trembled, distorting the shape of the people opposite. We stood back and watched in amazement as, one by one, the devotees lined up and walked calmly over the coals, their bare feet breaking through the crust of white ash, leaving behind the trace of glowing red footprints.

I was surprised to see the teenage son of English friends joining in the ceremony. He had a short pole inserted through both his cheeks, and he calmly walked the entire length of the fire without flinching as my sister took yet more photographs.

The mesmerising music continued. At the end of the firepit, priests waited to receive the walkers as they stepped off the glowing embers. They were held by the arms, and their poles were removed by twisting and pulling. There was no bleeding, and there seemed to be no discomfort as the poles and hooks were ceremoniously removed. The resulting wounds were neat vertical slits in the skin, which were then roughly daubed with ash. These men and women appeared to be released from trance at this point, and simply drifted into the crowd.

The music, which had been going on incessantly for hours, suddenly stopped, but unfortunately, there was a walker still in the centre of the firepit. He immediately came out of his trance-like state and started roaring in pain as he put his hands up and held the pole inserted through his cheeks. He appeared to suddenly feel the hot coals on his feet and started running in an attempt to leave the pit. Several men rushed to his side to support and hold him, but he struggled away, screaming and thrashing around.

The priest realised what was happening and tried to remove the pole from the afflicted man's cheeks, but unfortunately, it would not pull free. The walker was roughly pushed down onto the ground. The attendants held his head and shoulders as the priest again gripped the pole, pulling upwards with two hands, straining as though he was removing a stake from the ground. I watched with horror as the man's cheeks stretched and bled profusely as, finally, the pole was jerked free. He was raised into a sitting position, and handfuls of ash were applied to the wounds. However, the blood kept gushing, mixing with the ash on his cheeks and running down onto his chest. He opened his mouth, and more blood spilled out. My sister was still taking photographs as he was lifted up by the attendants and carried past us. I looked down and saw the exposed soles of his feet, they were blackened with ash but also badly burnt, red raw. I felt sick. He was quickly taken to the back of the temple, out of sight – I hoped he could be helped.

Concerned by what we had seen, Val sought out the young English boy and asked if she could check the soles of his feet. He smiled and obliged, they were dirty and covered in ash, but we were relieved to see they were not burnt or blistered. There were neat ash-daubed slits in each cheek where the pole had been removed, but he assured us that there was no pain, and I could see that they were not bleeding. He told us that he had come with friends from school, who had told him that it wouldn't hurt, and it hadn't. He explained that some people participated in the walk to fulfil a vow or to make a wish, but he had come to gain luck for his exams. My sister asked him what his parents thought about him firewalking. He laughed and said they didn't know yet but would probably kill him when they found out!

I wanted to go home, I had seen enough, but my sister's new friend insisted we stay for the celebratory meal. We followed him and sat on woven mats on the floor, eating with our fingers from banana leaf plates as delicious combinations of vegetarian curries, dahls, rice and chutney were ladled from metal buckets.

At last, we could go home. We thanked Val's gentleman friend and left.

The whole experience had been overwhelming on a sensory level, the noise, the heat, the incense, the crowd and what we had witnessed. How could we have seen what we had seen that day? I struggled to understand. I had so many questions and no answers. Was it the power of the mind over the body? Val told me that she had felt drawn into the crowd by the music, and the sensation she felt there had been similar to the sensation she experienced during hypnosis at her hospital weight loss sessions.

I had seen a hypnotist show many years earlier as a student. I hadn't liked it and hadn't been convinced then that it was real. This hypnotist had instructed the people on stage to do silly things and made them look ridiculous to entertain the audience. Volunteers had quacked like ducks and bitten into raw onions or lemons with apparent enjoyment, 'believing' they were eating apples or pears. People behaved in silly, embarrassing, or inappropriate ways for the hypnotist that I felt they would probably not have done ordinarily, all in the name of entertainment. I hadn't felt that the hypnosis or trance was real then, but now, I would have to re-think it. If trance was real and powerful enough to allow a person to walk in bare feet on hot coals without being burnt, then I wondered, how could the power of trance be used for good, in a way to make positive change, rather than just for entertainment?

A year later, on leave from Malaysia, I visited my sister in England and was invited to join her weight loss group to observe the hypnosis. I went along. I watched the ladies prepare for the dreaded weigh-in. Off came their shoes, tights, jumpers, underskirts, jewellery, false teeth, and hair clips. Some ladies hadn't eaten or drunk anything all day. If anyone had put on weight, then the consequence was that they had to change into a swimsuit and wear a large ugly pink paper-mâché pig's head for the rest of the session. These ladies would do anything to avoid this humiliation. Thankfully, on that day, all had lost weight, and no one had to endure the shame of the pig head. I was uncomfortable with the shaming consequence, and I wondered what would happen when the ladies finished with the group and the hypnosis, would their weight return?

The psychologist began the session by inducing trance collectively in the group, and out of interest, I tried to join in – but my eyes stayed firmly open. I watched as the rest of the group and my sister sat deep in trance. The psychologist went around the group, gently touching each lady on the shoulder, using her name, and listing the things she would no longer want to eat or drink, such as pies, chips, cakes, chocolate, and milk stout. He then instructed that if they did try to consume any of these items, they would feel physically ill and want to vomit. At this point, the ladies were dry retching and covering their mouths with their hands, still in deep trance.

This psychologist was a well-respected practitioner who worked at the local hospital. He was scheduled to talk to another ladies' group the following week, and he invited my sister and I to attend. We decided to go – I was intrigued and interested to learn more.

The following week, the psychologist explained how the unconscious mind worked. He described unbelievable case histories, and the results he claimed to obtain with hypnosis seemed miraculous.

After a break, he asked if anyone would like to volunteer to be hypnotised for a demonstration. There was great unease in the room. Ladies looked away, delved in handbags, went to the bathroom, stirred their tea, and giggled nervously.

I heard myself say, "I will."

Then I thought, "What have I done?"

I knew that I had not responded to his hypnotic suggestions during the group induction the previous week, and I was worried that nothing would happen this time and that his demonstration would be ruined.

The psychologist thanked me for volunteering and indicated that I should sit down at the front. I walked forward, already regretting volunteering, as an expectant silence filled the room.

He began. "Make yourself comfortable and look up at a spot on the ceiling."

I looked up and concentrated on a spot.

He spoke in a slow deep voice, "And… now, as I count from one to seven, you will find your eyes getting heavier and heavier, tireder and tireder. One… sleep… two… sleep… three… sleep… four… sleep… five… sleep… six… sleep… seven… sleep."

Nothing was happening, and I was getting embarrassed, so I decided to shut my eyes and focus on his words. I hoped he wouldn't try to make me do anything silly because I knew I would refuse.

"Now," he said. "Find yourself drifting back to a really happy time in your childhood."

Big mistake! I'd had a miserable childhood.

I tried to think of something happy.

It was then that I found myself sobbing uncontrollably out loud.

Tears were running down my face. I was aware that I was in a room with strangers, and I could hear my sister at the back of the room saying, "Oh my God!"

"… And why are you sad?" he went on.

"Because he's not my dog". I sobbed. My voice was that of my younger self, I could hear it, and I was astounded.

When I was about nine years old, our neighbour had a beautiful black and white spaniel called Spot. Spot loved me, and I loved him. Spot would meet me at my gate each school morning, and he would cross the road and wait with me for the bus. When I got on the bus, he would cross the road again safely and go home. In the afternoon, Spot would be faithfully waiting for me when I got off the bus, and we would walk home together. In that room, surrounded by strangers, I could smell his doggy smell and feel his silky ears. I sobbed some more.

"And what is making you cry?"

"He isn't my dog," I sobbed.

But, I had told everyone at school that Spot was my dog, and some girls had seen him from the bus. It was the biggest lie I had ever told. It was such a big lie that I couldn't ever have any friends home to play with. What if someone asked my sister about Spot? My friends had ponies and dogs and cats. All I had was a budgie called Nicky, it was not the same.

"And… can't you have a dog of your own?"

"No! Daddy says it will make a mess in the garden."

Part of me knew that I was a grown woman sitting there in that room, but part of me was my younger self breaking my heart over a dog I hadn't given a thought to for over thirty years.

"Do you have a dog now?" he asked gently.

"Yes," I sobbed.

He counted slowly to seven again, and I knew I had to open my eyes. I was dreading it.

My eyes opened to mayhem. Some of the ladies were in tears for the child with the dog. Others began to argue about the benefits of letting a child have a dog. Some seemed embarrassed, but not as embarrassed as I was. I was distraught and couldn't stop crying over Spot. My sister came and rescued me and took me home.

That experience, although confronting, had got me hooked. Through hypnosis, an animal I had not thought about for decades had become so real that I could smell him, feel his silky ears, and break my heart for my loss and the lie I had told.

I needed to know more about hypnosis, but I also needed to know how it could be used ethically, with careful consideration, and for good.

Years later, when I returned to the UK from Malaysia, I enrolled on a hypnotherapy training course with the Institute of Curative Hypnotherapists. On the first day, I was given a script to read to a willing subject. The script was designed to put someone into a trance. The person I was reading to, to my complete astonishment, went immediately into a deep trance. Her face went slack, her breathing slowed, and her eyes began moving from side to side behind her eyelids. Unfortunately, I had yet to be given page two! I left the poor lady slumped in her chair and rushed off in a panic to find the tutor. I didn't know what to do next.

After passing two training courses with distinction, I knew there was still a lot to learn. I attended more courses from world-renowned therapists, Norman Vaughton from the UK, Ernest Rossi from the USA, and David Grove from New Zealand. The more I learnt and experienced, the more I felt compelled to learn. Eventually, I was to become a Foundation Course Trainer for the Academy of Curative Hypnotherapists.

I set up a private practice which initially took time to establish. Some of the clients who came to see me had spent years previously in counselling, traditional therapy or on medication. To some, I really was the last resort, and they came with little hope after everything else had failed.

Over time I came to realise that I didn't have the answers to my client's problems. What I did have, though, was the ability to ask the right questions at the right time and in the right way. I was able, through hypnosis, to help my client access relevant memories to help them understand the cause of their problem and to change their beliefs, thinking, and behaviours in a way that was safe and beneficial to them. Some results were life changing.

By word of mouth, my practice thrived, and I was invited to talk to different businesses and social groups. Demand grew, and I was joined by a retired nurse who had trained in hypnotherapy, and a retired doctor, who had used hypnosis in his surgery for years. We all worked slightly differently, so we had various skills to offer our clients. Over time we witnessed many lives being transformed.

I started receiving referrals from health professionals who had become aware that the hypnotherapy sessions had really helped some of their patients and I was invited to talk to professional groups.

After a few years, my private practice became well-established, and I was given the opportunity to work as a part-time therapist in the Drug and Alcohol Department of the National Health Service. I had great success working with people withdrawing from benzodiazepines, I could use my hypnotherapy skills with surprising results. It made a lot of sense to me to get people off their medications and to work through what had been happening in their lives when they first felt they couldn't manage without being medicated.

Then an opening came up in Psychology, and I was fortunate enough to be given free rein with the full support of my manager. I started working there full-time and became a Senior Psychological Therapist.

I respected my colleagues. I had no Psychology degree, and I am sure I was a mystery to the many assistants I had to supervise as they had undertaken many years of university study and placements and passed many exams. I made certain that these assistants had all the clinical guidance they needed from qualified psychologists. But, I hoped that from sitting in on my sessions with clients, they realised the importance of the interaction between client and clinician, of using the right words and even of valuing silence. Silence is the space between words where meaningful change can happen.

After retiring, I emigrated to Australia and now live with my family on a beautiful island in the Pacific Ocean. However, even now, more than ten years later, I vividly remember client sessions word for word. My head is full to capacity, and thinking back, I continue to find some of the sessions and the outcomes so extraordinary that I believe they should be shared while I still remember them.

This book is a record of some of those sessions and the clients who trusted me with their experiences and came to me for help. Out of respect for them, I have chosen to protect their identities. Their stories, however, are all true.

1

THE MAN WHO CRIED

I knew he cried. He had been referred to Psychology because he couldn't stop crying.

It seemed from the referral letter that he was happily married, had two happy healthy children, enjoyed his job, and did a lot of sports and adventurous activities with the family.

So, I was interested to meet him and find out why he couldn't stop crying. He was sitting in the waiting room holding hands with his wife. I introduced myself and asked if she would like to join us. He shook his head.

We went through to the consulting room, he simply sat, leant forward with his arms on his thighs, his head down and the tears began to stream silently down his face, his shirt and even onto the carpet. I handed him a box of tissues and asked him if he would like a cup of tea. He looked up and nodded.

As we drank our tea, I said it must be difficult to come and talk to a stranger about his problem. He nodded again. I told him I knew that he had seen someone from work, then his doctor, then a counsellor and a psychiatrist and he'd been prescribed medication for depression.

"I'm not depressed." He said, "I just can't stop crying."

"I see." I said. "This would be easier to sort out if you knew why you cry, but my guess is that you don't know."

He agreed. "Everyone keeps asking me that question, but I don't know the answer."

His councillor had told him that if he didn't stop crying, his wife would get fed up and leave him. So now he had uncontrollable crying and also the terror of being abandoned by his wife. Understandably, he didn't want to see that councillor again.

After a while, he started talking about his wife. She had been his childhood sweetheart. They had been together from school and married as soon as they could. They had two wonderful children, who were doing well at school with good friends and lots of interests. Both were sporty and musical. The elder was planning to go to university soon and they were proud of them both.

My client felt his job security was under threat because he felt compelled to phone his wife every ten minutes from work, to ask her if she was going to leave him. She would always answer, "No." She would tell him where she was when he rang, cleaning the bathroom, or shopping at the supermarket and they would discuss what to have for tea. He would return to his work, but the feelings of distress and abandonment would soon begin to build up again and he would be back on the phone looking for reassurance. His wife never complained, she was always supportive and would tell him she loved him and would never leave him.

I said that for such a happy man with such a good family and life it seemed extraordinary he felt the way he did, and that the crying would not be silenced.

I explained how I could work with him using hypnosis, almost as though I was the therapist for the tears, because the tears would know what it was all about, even if he did not. He was interested.

He told me he thought he had always been sad. When he was young, his parents had told him that he was adopted as a baby. He had been loved and well cared for, he had older siblings, but he was aware that he didn't look like any of them. The other children were bright and did well at school and he really struggled with reading and writing, however hard he tried. His adoptive parents were supportive, they showed no disappointment in him, but he felt as though he had let them down.

It was the end of our session, and I asked him if he could come back the following week. He said he wanted to. He felt hopeful that at last, he could be helped. I gave him a relaxation CD to listen to, to get him used to my voice. The CD included positive suggestions as, *'helping you to be as you want to be'*, and *to 'feel as you want to feel'*, and *'Your story can be told in a way that it is safe for you, so that there can be those changes and all the difference that difference makes'.*

He agreed to play it. I told him it could make him fall asleep, or it might annoy him, or he could find that he learnt the words like memorising a song, just from hearing it repeated often.

His poor wife looked concerned but smiled when he went back to her in the waiting room, and he hugged her and said he would be coming back to see me the following week.

So, the next week came, and he arrived for the appointment alone. The first thing I noticed was that he wasn't crying! He informed me that he had played the CD every night, but hadn't even heard it because it made him fall asleep! He'd had the best week at work, and now just phoned his wife at lunchtimes. His eyes were bright, he sat up straight and said he wanted to talk to me about how he had always felt that he didn't belong with his adoptive family. He loved them and appreciated all they had done for him, but had always longed to find his real mother. I asked if he had ever tried to contact her, and he said he didn't know how to go about it.

I certainly hadn't done any such investigation myself, but instead of a cup of tea, this time, I went and got my mobile phone. I rang the Salvation Army. They were very helpful. We learnt it was possible to trace people if those people were agreeable to be traced. They offered to send someone to see my client, to discuss his options in further detail.

An arrangement was made for a lady to visit him at home. He would be contacted in the next few days. Phone numbers were exchanged. He was told that all records were kept centrally, and if he wished to go ahead, they could start requesting his details.

He left in a haze, of hope and the possibility of finally finding his birth mother. He rang me during the week to let me know his details had been taken and the Salvation Army had started making enquiries on his behalf. He sounded so optimistic, but also let me know that he had not shared what he was doing with his adoptive family as he was concerned that it might hurt their feelings and he did not wish to seem ungrateful.

He came back for his appointment the following week. They had found his mother. They contacted her, and she'd been very emotional and revealed she had never wanted to give him up, but had been given no other choice. She also said she had never stopped thinking about him.

His mother was now married. Her husband was not his father, but knew about him, as did his three half siblings. He was amazed to hear they all celebrated his birthday every year.

He was asked if he wished to meet his mother.

"Yes!"

The Salvation Army organised the meeting at a hotel halfway between their two towns. He took his wife, and his mother took her husband. My client invited me to go too. I politely declined, I felt my part in his journey was over, but I would be thinking about him.

He came back the following week. He brought with him a baby coat his mother had knitted for him when she was pregnant, along with precious letters and cards kept by the adoption agency that she had written to him throughout the years. His mother had never stopped loving and thinking about him. I must admit that it was my client who was handing me the tissues this time.

His mother told him her story. She came from a very poor strict Irish Catholic family. Her father was a docker when he could find work, and her mother looked after the house and children. There was no happiness, just never-ending chores to do and wearing hand-me-down clothes.

She had been fifteen when the fair came to town. She arranged to go with her friends. The girls got ready together and they went out to have the time of their lives.

They got a lot of attention from groups of boys but only one boy caught her eye. He ran the dodgems. He laughed and had lovely eyes and gave her free rides all evening and when it got late and her friends left to go home, she stayed with the dodgem boy.

As the fair closed, she knew she would be in trouble for being home late, but she still didn't care. She went with him behind the stalls, and he kissed her. She had never felt like this. His hands moved all over her and it felt wonderful. They made love to the music and sounds of the fair. It was glorious. She had never felt so loved, so special in all her life. She had fallen in love.

Then she had to go home.

She got in terrible trouble for being late, but didn't care.

The next night despite being grounded, she went out again to meet him, but the streets were dark and deserted. The fair had gone. Her heart was broken, she had to go home.

Sometime later she felt unwell. It was her mother who worked out why she was ill in the mornings. How had something that seemed so glorious suddenly become dirty, sinful, and wrong? Her parents were disgusted and ashamed of her. The priest was called in. It was arranged that she would be sent immediately to "visit and care for an auntie who was unwell". There was no auntie. She was instead sent in disgrace to a Catholic Home for 'naughty girls.'

The Home was in another town, and no one came to visit her. The girls slept in dormitories and worked hard, cleaning, washing and ironing. Pregnant girls came and went and there was a lot of crying. It was never explained to her what was to happen at the birth or afterwards.

Her time to give birth came. Things were not going well. It was a complicated labour, and she was in a lot of pain, eventually, she had to go to hospital in an ambulance. She was later told that both she and the baby had nearly died.

After the difficult birth, her baby boy was ill. She nursed him and as she held him to her breast, and looked into his beautiful eyes, she fell completely in love with him. She was at the hospital and then in a nursing home for about six weeks until he grew stronger. Then the day came when the nuns arrived with an ultimatum. If she went home without the baby her father would allow her to return, but the matter was never to be spoken of again. If she kept the baby, then she would have no home, no family, no money, and no support.

She had no choice; they took her baby away and she felt broken. She went home alone.

She told my client that he had cried as he was taken from her and that the overwhelming grief that she had felt at having to give him up, had stayed with her until this day.

He told me that when they met they had hugged each other, and they had both cried.

"But this time," he said. "They were happy tears."

My client went on later to meet the rest of his extended family. He looked like them, and his mother told him he had his father's beautiful eyes. He finally belonged.

He had since spoken to his adoptive family and told them he had found and met up with his birth mother. They were happy for him, and they were to all meet up soon.

So why had he cried?

I understood the "not belonging" but what had been the catalyst that made these tears flow so relentlessly at this time in his life when he was a happily married man with his own children?

He closed his eyes, then he said, "I think it's to do with my daughter."

I asked him what he meant.

He explained.

His family had always done everything together, until one day his fifteen-year-old daughter had come to him and innocently asked if she could go to the fair with her friends. She promised that she wouldn't be home late. He agreed, she was a sensible girl, her friends were reliable, and he knew she was growing up and one day soon she would leave for university.

She went to the fair and at that point, his world came crashing down and the tears began. It made absolutely no sense to him, but it must have made sense on a deeper level to an unconscious part of him. Where does memory live? I don't know. However, he had now found the answer to the question, "Why are you crying?" – he understood it, and he no longer needed to cry.

He thanked me for listening, and for putting him in touch with the Salvation Army who had helped him to find his mother. He said his wife was so grateful to have her husband back, and he said as he left, jokingly,

"My wife thinks you must have put something in the tea!"

Footnote

I asked myself – how did my client overcome this problem? I hadn't even hypnotised him. He said he believed the change came when he played the CD, even though he couldn't remember any of the words. It was as though a door had opened for him that had been shut forever. He asked if he could keep the CD to play, "just in case."

I think it must have been sheer coincidence that his daughter asking to go to the fair became the trigger for his uncontrollable crying and fear of abandonment. The fair story was not his, it was his mother's. Would the same reaction have been triggered by a simple request from his daughter to go dancing or to the movies? Possibly. I don't know and I didn't need to know. What mattered to me was that my client was finally able to understand the cause of the problem and move on from this traumatic phase.

In conventional therapy my client might have received counselling for anxiety and perhaps been given coping mechanisms or medication to overcome his symptoms. He could have continued crying for many years with terrible consequences for his health, work, and family.

What he needed instead, was to be able to understand the origins of his extreme distress, and fear of abandonment, which went back to the trauma he experienced as a baby when he was removed from his loving mother. By reuniting with his mother, he was made whole and the abandonment issue and crying problem resolved itself and he was able to return to his own loving family, secure in the knowledge of who he was.

2

I HATE TUESDAYS

I wasn't quite sure what to expect from my next client. I'd been asked to see her urgently following her discharge from the psychiatric ward, where she had been placed after taking an overdose. Her referral notes revealed that she was seventeen and had been living with her addict boyfriend, who had just been arrested and jailed for selling drugs. She'd overdosed on pills, cut her wrists and had only just been found in time.

I wondered if she was an addict too, did she feel that he was the love of her life, did she feel that she couldn't live without him and was she still suicidal?

What a pleasant surprise walked into my consulting room. She was young, healthy-looking, well-dressed, polite, and beautiful! She told me that she was relieved to be out of the psychiatric ward and felt she would have gone insane if she'd stayed there any longer. However, she'd only been permitted to leave the ward on the understanding that she lived at home with her parent's support and that she agreed to come and see me. At this time, we had a huge waiting list for clients of up to four years, so someone must have felt she needed to be seen immediately. I later found out that it was a hospital psychiatrist who had been to a talk I'd given some months earlier who had recommended that my client be fast-tracked to see me.

She was easy to talk to and I was surprised to find out that she had never taken drugs. Her boyfriend sold drugs to fund his addiction, but she didn't like what he did. They lived in a flat in a dangerous part of town where other addicts would come to buy drugs from him and she would lock herself in the bathroom until they left.

"What is it about your boyfriend that makes you prepared to live like this?" I asked.

"Is it love?"

"No."

"Is it for the money?"

"No."

I didn't understand and I asked her to explain.

She replied that she had never had a boyfriend before and when he'd asked her to move in with him she agreed because she felt that she would never be asked by anyone else. Her parents were distraught and had asked her to come home, but she was determined to stay with him. They didn't go anywhere or do anything together. They hardly spoke. He went on his PlayStation, drank alcohol, sold drugs, and watched videos.

"Why did you overdose when he was arrested?" I asked.

"Because I was scared that no other boy would ever want me," she replied.

I asked her if she would be interested to hear about hypnotherapy – which was one way I could work with her. I explained there are two parts to the mind, the conscious and the unconscious. The conscious mind tends to be rational and critical, making decisions and forming opinions. The unconscious mind deals with feelings, emotions, memories, dreams, and past experiences. I told her that experiencing the hypnotic state was a bit like being in a daydream when you're aware of where you are, but when memories appear it may seem as though you're reliving the experience at the age at which it occurred.

She was interested to work with me in this way, so we made an appointment for the following week. In the meantime, she was to keep living at home with her parents.

The following week she arrived looking stunning, with fashionably cut shiny hair, well-applied makeup, leather boots and jacket – she looked like a model.

She made herself comfortable in the reclining chair and I started the induction, she readily accepted my suggestions and was soon in a deep trance.

... Drifting back in time to the cause of the problem or something relating to the cause of the problem... my voice was low and slow.

"It's Tuesday – I hate Tuesdays," came a much younger voice.

What is it about Tuesday's that you hate?

"It's sport. I hate sport at this school. At my old school, I was always top of the class, I was good at everything. I was on a lot of teams, and I was a good runner and swimmer. I even liked doing homework. I loved my old school."

Wow, that does sound like a good school.

"Yes, it was. Then I had to leave that school and go to the senior school. My best friends didn't get into this school, so I didn't see them much, but I made new friends and worked hard. I was always top or near the top of my class, but it all changed."

But it all changed... and how did it change?

"Well, girls started getting boobs. Some girls liked them, and some girls hated them. The boys teased the girls with boobs and tried to touch them. Those girls went around together for safety when they could. I waited and waited to get my boobs, but nothing ever happened. Mum bought me some padded bras and I felt better. I felt like everyone else."

"Then we got a new sports teacher with hairy legs. She liked hockey and we played it every Tuesday. Playing hockey was sweaty and muddy and she said we all had to strip off and shower together afterwards. She would stand there and watch. I refused to shower; I did not want to take off my bra because then everyone would know about my boobs. We argued and I got detention. So, I stopped staying at school on Tuesdays. I'd go in the morning, register, and then leave. Sometimes if I knew that Mum was out, I would go home, but that was risky. Sometimes I went to the library, but I would get funny looks because of my school uniform. Sometimes I'd go around the shops, but people stared, so I took clothes with me and changed in the toilets. I was not so noticeable out of uniform."

"Then Wednesdays came, because I had no note explaining my Tuesday absence, my parents were contacted, and they were furious. Because I missed Tuesdays, I got behind at school and my grades dropped – my parents couldn't understand it. Every day became a bad day, so I decided not to bother going to school any more. I was in trouble with everyone."

"Being on the streets in summer was not too bad, but it was dreadful in winter. It was really cold, so I found a café where I could sit all day with a drink if I wanted to. I read library books and met some older girls at the café. They were not from my school and eventually, we became friends, like being in a gang. I knew it was bad, but I felt like I belonged. I joined in when they went shoplifting. I was scared, but I didn't stop. One girl would bring along her sister's baby in a pram, which was a really good way of hiding things we stole. I took small stuff like makeup and sweets. They were braver and started taking electrical things and clothes. The café was a way of getting rid of things, swapping them, or selling them. I didn't do that. I couldn't take anything big home because I wouldn't have been able to explain it."

"Sometimes we got chased. Some girls got caught. It scared us, but we didn't stop. When we became recognised in the local shops, we took a bus to the next town and started stealing again. I became good at distracting the assistants while the others stole.

"I'm not sure how it changed from stealing from shops to robbing things from cars, but it did. Then it moved on to robbing the cars themselves. I don't know what the girls did with the cars, they were all older than me."

"I couldn't take my school exams, so I got no qualifications. I got a part-time job as a cleaner and worked in a laundrette and a fish and chip shop. Then one day in the café, I met him. He sat with me, and I felt special. When he asked me to move in with him I agreed, but I was scared.

What were you scared of?

"That he would find out."

That he would find out what?

She started sobbing, "That I have no boobs! Then he would get rid of me or tell everyone."

I reassured her... *that was then but this is now. Just because that was the way it used to be, does not mean that it always has to be that way.*

I gave my client positive suggestions about acknowledging her problem and finding positive ways to take the next step forward. She listened, stopped sobbing and when she was calm, I brought her out of trance.

When she opened her eyes, she was surprised at what had just happened and embarrassed to have shared her past with me. She said she'd felt younger and vividly remembered the anxiety of stealing and nearly being caught. She then told me it wasn't that she had small boobs but that she had no boobs at all. Her body was like that of a young girl. I asked her about her boyfriend and how he had felt about her body. It seemed that he'd never noticed and never mentioned anything. He was usually drunk or high and just wanted to be seen with a pretty girl.

"Have you ever discussed this with your doctor?" I asked.

"No. It's too embarrassing and we couldn't afford plastic surgery anyway. Mum just buys me padded bras"

I asked her who her doctor was. It turned out that I knew him and had spoken to him on previous occasions regarding other clients. I asked my client for permission to ring him on her behalf. She nodded. Amazingly I got through straight away. I explained who I was, who I had with me and what the problem was. The doctor listened and went quiet and then apologised for not having picked up on her developmental problem, he had never realised.

"Could she come to see me this afternoon?" he asked.

She agreed.

At her request, I asked about operations and costs. He said he believed that this would not be considered a cosmetic procedure as it was instead treatment to rectify a medical condition that had been missed. My client left feeling brave and optimistic.

She phoned me later. The doctor had referred her to a specialist and her Mum was going to go with her. The appointment came through quickly and after seeing the specialist, she rang again to let me know that an appointment had been made for the augmentation operation and that there was to be no charge. I advised her to be realistic in choosing her new breast size to fit her frame and to treat her new body with great respect. She remained on my client list and could contact me if she needed another appointment, but I knew that her focus now was on the medical procedure.

Some months later the receptionist phoned to say that my client had arrived and asked if she could see me. I agreed. She looked radiant, had brought flowers and had come to thank me. She had also come to show me something – lifting her T-shirt, under which there was no bra, to display a beautiful pair of perfectly formed breasts!

"Well, that's a first!" I said. "And are you happy?"

"Oh yes!" she smiled.

She was still living with her parents and had gone to college, catching up on the subjects not completed at school. She was doing well and enjoying the challenge and had a part-time job with a bookie, and loved the numbers, the odds, and the banter with the punters. She hugged me on leaving and thanked me again.

I heard no more from her until years later when a postcard of the Eiffel Tower arrived from Paris letting me know that she had successfully gained her qualifications, undertaken further training, and was working in financial services in London. She was away for a weekend in Paris and wanted to thank me again and let me know how good her life was now. I was so pleased to have been able to help her achieve her full potential and recognise her own worth.

Footnote

I often wonder if that sports teacher was ever aware of the damage she'd caused my client by attempting to force a teenage girl with body issues into a communal school shower. The fear of exposure, literally and psychologically, was so great that my client had chosen to drop out of the school where she excelled rather than be naked in front of her peers. Not even her own mother had realised this was the underlying cause of her truancy, despite knowing that her daughter had a developmental problem.

My client was lucky to have been referred so quickly, and hypnosis provided the perfect conduit to allow her to reveal the problem with her breasts and to help me to help her to do something practical about it. For my client, breast augmentation was quite literally life changing.

Sometimes when an overwhelming secret must be kept, such as "I have no boobs" it's impossible to get this information from the client's rational, conscious mind through talking – it has been too big a secret for too long a period of time. Through hypnosis, my client could go directly to the root of the problem and communicate this to me in a way that the rational, conscious mind would not have been able to. Under hypnosis, the unconscious mind gets through the blocks and safety walls that the conscious mind has put up to protect the person. Hypnosis allowed the cause of the problem to be safely revealed, explained, and then subsequently successfully addressed.

3

SMOKING IS MY ONLY COMFORT

This time it was a doctor from the hospital who wanted me to work with his patient. The lady was in her late twenties and was married with five young children. She was in very poor health and had a serious lung problem which had been scheduled for surgery and had been told to stop smoking before the hospital was prepared to proceed with the operation. There were concerns the anaesthetic would be too dangerous. The procedure had been cancelled three times already as she'd been unable to give up the habit. A new date had been set, and my client had already informed the hospital she'd given up smoking (she hadn't), but she couldn't wait any longer, as soon she would be too ill to have the operation.

She'd tried to give up cigarettes many times before and failed. The doctor, realising that his patient was still smoking, had sent her to see me in the hope that hypnosis might help.

She arrived looking thin, pale, tired and very worried. She coughed constantly. Her husband was a long-distance lorry driver, he was often away from home for weeks at a time, and she was exhausted from looking after their children on her own. She never ate meals with the children, and the only time she had for herself was when they were finally in bed, and she could relax at the end of the day with her 'smokes'. Smoking was her only comfort.

She told me that she bought cheap cigarettes when she could afford them but usually rolled her own.

"I have to smoke," she told me. "I don't know what I'd do if I couldn't, but I know I have to stop. I need to have the operation for my kids, for myself – I don't want to die," she sobbed. "Smoking makes me feel better, but I feel so guilty when I do it."

My client said that the cigarettes helped to relieve her cough. I explained that the cigarettes contained tar and toxins, and when she inhaled, the tar glued down the mucus in her lungs, temporarily stopping her coughing. It might seem as though it was helping, but it was actually causing her more harm. She was surprised, but it made sense to her.

I discussed hypnotherapy and how we could work together. I explained I was going to help her to become a non-smoker rather than make her give up cigarettes. I said that the process would be similar to people who had decided to cut out sugar from their tea. At first, the tea would taste terrible, but with perseverance, they would soon learn to enjoy the tea's flavour and would never need to use sugar again. She nodded and said that she knew a friend who had done this.

We were under great pressure to make this session work. My client had to be ready to have this operation – it was her last chance.

I asked her if she had any cigarettes with her. She seemed surprised but got out a packet and handed me one. I held it and asked her to sit back and relax in the chair. I induced trance, she responded well and was soon receptive to my suggestions, but she continued to cough.

I told her that whenever she tried to smoke in the future, she would feel as though the whole cigarette was as hot as the burning tip. She smiled, and curious, I asked her why she was smiling.

"Coz I reckon I'm quick enough to take a drag before it burns me, then put it down!" she replied.

Your lips are very soft and tender, and as soon as the cigarette touches your lips, they will feel burnt.

She smiled again and said, "It'd still be worth it!"

So, I passed her the unlit cigarette, but I told her it was lit.

She appeared to feel heat as she held the cigarette. She juggled it, passing it quickly from hand to hand, putting it closer to her mouth. She finally put it to her lips and inhaled deeply, before gasping and throwing the cigarette to the floor. She clutched her mouth with both hands and moaned as if in pain.

I ignored the coughing and moaning and carried on with the therapy, giving positive suggestions such as,

You will soon get your taste back and enjoy much more, the foods and flavours that you haven't been able to enjoy for a very long time.

Your lungs will cough up all the mucus that has been stuck inside – but this is also good! Let your lungs cough. They are taking this opportunity to clean themselves. You will enjoy inhaling good, fresh air to cleanse your lungs.

You will feel so proud of yourself. Just think what this change will mean to your children and husband. Just think of what you will be able to do with all the money that you will save. Imagine how much healthier you and your family will be.

I reminded her, *your lips will remember the pain of the burning cigarette, and your lips do not want to feel this pain.* (She moaned again).

As you become a non-smoker, you will avoid this pain and be happier and healthier.

Your lips, lungs and whole body will be happy to become and remain a non-smoker.

When you have accepted all these changes, then, and only then, your eyes will open into the here and now, my words staying with you and working with you… and all the difference this difference makes.

I sat in silence and waited. After some minutes, my client finally opened her eyes and sat up. Her hands were still cupped over her mouth, and when she removed them, I was shocked but didn't react. I couldn't believe what I was seeing.

Her lips were enormous, swollen, red and blistered, just as though they had been burnt!

I was horrified and hoped my insurance would cover me for inflicting a burn on a client through suggestion. It looked like a cosmetic procedure that had gone badly wrong! I didn't even know if it was possible for a real burn to have reacted so dramatically in that time. Under hypnosis, my client's unconscious mind had literally accepted my suggestions and produced the blisters she believed she would have sustained following a burn from the unlit cigarette.

She looked at me and spoke with difficulty through her swollen, blistered lips.

"That's wonderful!" she mumbled.

She left disfigured and in pain but a happy non-smoker.

I told her she could contact me if she needed to, but I didn't hear from her for quite some time. I wondered if I was going to be sued.

A few weeks later, I got a phone call from my client's mother, who told me her daughter had finally gone in for her operation. She had moved into her daughter's house to look after her grandchildren, and another daughter was coming through during the day to help, bringing her children too. Chaos!

I asked her how my client was doing. Her mother said she had come home from seeing me in a "hell of a mess" but was extremely happy and had not smoked a cigarette since. Evidently, she couldn't stand the smell of cigarettes now and had washed all her clothes when she got home and insisted that her mother and sister go outside to smoke. Mum sounded concerned and said she didn't know how her son-in-law would cope when he returned home, as he, too, was a heavy smoker. She said her daughter was even talking about redecorating because the ceilings were a mess, stained brown from nicotine.

"Will she return to normal soon because she's a pain to live with?" her mother asked.

"Your daughter will continue to concentrate on improving her own and her family's health and well-being," I replied.

"Bloody Hell!" said her mother.

I finally heard from my client when she returned home after the successful operation, she felt she'd been given a second chance at life and was determined to make the most of it for herself and her family. She was enjoying eating apples again after years of not being able to taste them. I asked about her lips. She said they had healed perfectly, and there was no lasting damage.

I breathed a silent sigh of relief. I'd learnt an important lesson – to never work by giving such potentially damaging instructions again during trance. I understood my client's necessity and urgency for giving up smoking, and I was working with her best interests at heart. The outcome was what she and the doctor had hoped for. She was now a non-smoker, able to have her operation, but never would I have intentionally given suggestions that would have inflicted pain and disfigurement.

Footnote

Some years later, I watched a documentary on the phenomenon of hypnosis. It showed a French therapist placing a cold coin onto a hypnotised woman's arm and telling her that the coin was hot. He lifted the cold coin to reveal a perfect circle of blistered skin underneath. I hadn't even known that this immediate reaction of the skin was possible until I saw my client and her blistered lips. It was interesting to see the blister inflicted intentionally.

I was extra cautious after this session with my client and never used such brutal suggestions in this way again. However, I did harness the power of suggestions to help other clients, but always with care, now that I knew what I said to clients in trance could be taken literally and manifest in such extraordinarily powerful ways.

Over many years of working with hypnosis, I did a lot of training with renowned teachers and therapists. I even allowed them to use me as a 'guinea pig' on occasions to demonstrate new techniques. I learnt so much from all these experiences, but I learnt most of all from my clients, as I learnt from them exactly what needed to happen for them to have the best positive outcome.

Counselling Psychotherapist David Grove found that questions which interfered with the client's experience the least were, in fact, the most effective in bringing about positive change. It is so true. I learnt from him the importance of 'Clean Language', which reduces the therapist's influence on the client, and I always tried to remember that a good therapist is only as good as their next question.

I have trained some doctors and dentists who wanted to use hypnosis for pain control or to help overcome patient anxiety and phobias. Many of these professionals initially found it difficult to relinquish their control of the situation and allow the patients to control their own solutions. However, once these medical professionals understood how to work differently in this way, many became very effective indeed.

Part of my work in the Psychology Department was to supervise psychology assistants. These assistants were part way through their training to becoming clinical psychologists. They were required to gain experience within various departments, including but not limited to Adult Mental Health, Learning Difficulties, the Elderly, and Children. These assistants were intense, dedicated and frighteningly intelligent – I sometimes wondered who the student was and who the teacher was!

With the permission of my clients, these psychology assistants could sit in on some of my sessions. I was constantly asked by the assistants how I knew what to do and what to say. My way of working with clients was so far removed from what they had been taught at university, and it was often challenging for them. But what I did with my clients worked.

One outstanding psychology assistant, Clare, consistently challenged and analysed my working methods, stating that she thought I was 'flying by the seat of my pants.' I was. I needed to. Each new client had individual needs that required a unique and personal response. Good effective therapy is not a one size fits all solution. Clare took on everything I could teach her and more and is now a highly respected and effective practitioner in her field.

A lot of what the psychology assistants had learnt up to this point was derived from secondary sources – from other people's work, papers, books and lectures. Through my use of 'Clean Language' in sessions, I could show the assistants first hand that the clients themselves often held the solution to their problem within them – the clients just did not know that they did. Using precisely the right words was everything.

I also taught psychology assistants that silence during therapy should not be feared or avoided. Silences were the valuable spaces between words where an active change occurred for the client.

It is essential for the therapist to be able to put one foot into the reality of the client but also imperative to keep one foot firmly in their own reality.

4

WARTS AND ALL

Within the Psychology Department, I worked specifically with adults referred with mental health problems, but it was in my private practice where some of my most interesting and unusual work happened. Here I had a much more diverse range of clients of both ages and symptoms who came because they wanted to, not because they had been sent.

My secretary had booked this next appointment. All I knew was that my client was a young boy with warts. Working with children was normally a pleasure because they had such wonderfully vivid imaginations that I could easily tap into and work with. They usually came with hope, belief and high expectations.

This boy arrived with his mother and was enclosed in a huge black puffer jacket. I could see legs but no hands or face, just eyes above the zipped-up snorkel hood, and I could see that his eyelids were covered in warts.

He was six years old and very withdrawn; his mother did all the talking. As he sat quietly, she told me they lived on a farm, where her son was a great help – he was especially good with the lambs in Spring. He spent most of his time outside and often rescued injured wild animals and birds, including a hedgehog. But now he hated going to school. I showed interest and asked him why he hated school.

Once again, his mother replied for him. "His friends won't play with him anymore. Since he's grown these warts, no one will sit with him or share with him. He doesn't even get chosen for teams anymore, which makes him sad because he's really good at sports."

"That sounds miserable," I said. "I understand now why you hate going to school. How long has it been like this?"

"About a year," said his mother. "And when it's time to leave for school, he runs away and hides."

"Do you think," I asked. "That if we could get rid of these warts, you could like school again?"

The hooded head nodded.

His mother explained that they had tried many times to remove the warts. Some had been frozen off by the doctor, but it had hurt, and they had regrown. They'd also tried painting 'stuff' on his warts, but that hadn't worked either. The warts always grew back.

I assured him the way I worked would not be painful in any way and that I didn't use 'stuff'.

"I have something else, something that is a bit like magic!" I said.

The hooded head looked up, and again I could see many warts around his eyelids, but his eyes were shining. He was interested. I simply explained hypnosis and said, "I will tell the warts to go away. If the warts were clever enough to grow in the first place, they're clever enough to know how to disappear. People's warts drop off all the time. We just want this to happen to your warts now, not later."

He nodded.

Getting his wart-covered hands out of the sleeves, I did a suggestibility test. I told him to stare at his index fingertips with his hands clasped together. I demonstrated. He followed my example. As I lowered my voice, I told him that he would find his fingers slowly beginning to close together, *closer and closer, nearer and nearer* until they touched. They did. He was entranced.

Then I told him his fingers were stuck together as though with very strong glue. He pulled and pulled, but they stayed firmly stuck together! Then I told him all the glue had gone away, and his fingers could open again – and they did! He and I were now on the same page – let's use this powerful magic on these warts!

I induced trance, and because I knew he lived on a farm and was interested in nature and saving animals, I took him on an imaginary walk, through green fields, past hedges and trees, noticing clouds, bird song and animals. I took him all the way to the edge of a beautiful pond, and there I told him that he could hear crying.

As you walk towards the pond carefully, look to see where the crying is coming from. It's coming from a toad! It's not just an ordinary toad. This toad can talk. Because you are such a kind and caring boy, and because you are so good with animals, you ask the toad, "Why are you crying?"

The toad tells you a very sad tale.

He is crying because no one will play with him.

When he goes near the pond, all the other toads move away. It's because he is different. This toad is not covered in warts like the other toads. He is smooth and does not have a single wart. All the other toads have huge lumpy warts, which make them very proud. The more warts they have, the better! The other toads show off their warts sitting by the side of the pond, croaking. This crying toad knows that he will never be able to join in with the other toads until he grows warts, but he doesn't know how to do this.

The boy pondered the problem.

I took a quick glance over at his mother and smiled – she stared at me but did not smile back.

There was a long pause... then a tiny voice from within the hood spoke.

"He can have all of mine!"

Are you sure? I asked. *If you give him all your warts, you won't have any left.*

"Yes!" he exclaimed.

I felt he thought I was stupid! He had found the perfect solution to both their problems. He would give all the warts he hated so much to the toad, and then they could both be happy.

Well, if you are sure... that is very kind of you.

I instructed him to go carefully to the edge of the pond, to bend down and put his hands in the water and wash them. I told him to rub his hands together gently, then rub his 'wet' hands over his eyelids and around his eyes. He pushed his hood back. This was the first time I had seen his face. This poor boy was covered in warts. He kept dipping his hands into the imaginary pond, then rubbing his ears, neck, arms, elbows, legs, knees – everywhere, all over his body, through the coat. Finally, he relaxed.

Are you sure that you have washed all of them? I asked.

"Yes," he said, relieved.

I continued.

The toad is still here, but he's stopped crying, and he sees what you're doing. The 'growing' parts of your warts are now floating in the water, and he jumps in. He puts his head and whole body under the water and splashes around. Then he gets out. He still has no warts, but we both know this magic takes time.

The same time it took for your warts to grow will be the same time needed for them to disappear. You have to be patient. I don't know if the warts will disappear one by one or all at once, nor do I know if the toad will grow all his warts one by one or all at once – but I do know that the warts know how to do it, and in a way that is just right for both of you.

Once this process has started… then and only then… for a happy handsome boy who will have no warts and a happy handsome toad who will be covered in warts, your eyes will open into the here and now… and the magic will begin!

We sat there in silence, waiting.

I took another glance at his mother, who looked very confused. Finally, her son opened his eyes, he smiled, and we could talk.

His mother told me that she didn't understand what had happened but revealed that her fingers had also stuck together during the suggestibility test and then had come apart as she listened to my words. She asked what would happen next for her son.

I replied that now we just needed to wait. The process would take as much time as it took.

I advised her she could contact me if she needed to. I also suggested to her son that the more often he washed or showered in the bathroom at home, the quicker the warts would go. I stressed that it had to be water from a tap, a bath, or a shower, not pond water (that was for the toad!), as I was worried about him washing in a pond on the farm and falling in. He was smiling as he left.

As I washed my hands I mused that two hundred years ago I would probably have been burnt as a witch! As children my mother had told us that the best way to get rid of a wart was to pull a hair from the tail of the milkman's patient horse. This hair would be tightly wound and tied around the offending wart until it eventually dropped off! Other people have told me how they had removed their warts by selling them to their grandpa for six pence! The belief that this would work was so strong, that no one was surprised when the wart fell off!

From previously witnessing the extraordinary reaction that my lady client had, where the mere suggestion of a lit cigarette had severely blistered her lips, I knew that hypnosis could have a powerful effect on the skin. Still, I'd never used it before to remove warts, and I was interested to see the outcome.

About a year later, I was contacted by the same mother. She informed me that her son had no warts. I felt elated and was keen to know more. She was ringing me to make an appointment because her five-year-old daughter was now covered in warts, and she wanted to bring her in for more of my 'magic.'

They arrived for their appointment. I think the girl was wearing the same black puffer jacket as her brother had worn, except because she was younger and smaller, it covered all of her head, most of her face and went down past her knees. I could see her sparkling eyes peering up at me from inside the hood. She already believed in the magic.

I explained that I would have to check because I might have already used up all the wart magic on her brother. Her mother looked confused. I went to my filing cabinet, opened a drawer, and looked in. The girl's eyes were nearly popping out of her head with anticipation as I pulled out an empty envelope and looked inside.

"This is definitely the envelope for wart magic, but I'm sorry, there doesn't seem to be enough left in here for a six-year-old girl," I said, shaking my head.

"But... I'm only five," she wailed, holding up five fingers.

"Oh, that's different then. That's so lucky. There's just enough in here for a five-year-old girl!" The girl looked relieved, and so did her mother.

I asked the girl if it would be all right to take off her jacket.

"Yes!"

Her mother helped, and everything came off, even her jeans, and she was left standing in her undies.

"Show me every wart," I said.

This child was covered in warts.

She had warts growing on warts. I put my fingers into my empty envelope and then touched every wart, on elbows, knees, ears, toes, between fingers – everywhere.

"Now, are you sure, absolutely sure, that's all of them?"

"Yes!" she said.

Her mother nodded.

Just as well, the envelope was empty – I showed her – empty! I crumpled it up and threw it into the bin. She got dressed. I told them it would take as long as it took, but the warts knew how to do this, and it wouldn't be long until she noticed they were all gone. As she left, she was a very happy five-year-old, and her mother was happy too.

Again, I went to the wash basin and washed my hands. Because the girl had been so young, I'd felt it was an important thing to do, to build anticipation by having just the right amount of magic in the envelope. It was also important for me to touch each of the warts that were so hated – as each one was given special attention and a dose of "magic," it had made the process tangible for the girl.

I did not need to formally induce trance with this five-year-old, as she was so ready to accept my suggestions. She already knew that my magic had worked for her brother's warts, and she believed in it totally because she'd seen the proof with her own eyes. Once again, I told the mother that she could contact me if she needed to, but I never heard back from her.

About a year later, in a shopping centre in a different town, I heard my name being called, and there was the mother with two friends on a shopping spree. I asked after her children, and she said her daughter's results had not been as good as her son's – I was sorry to hear this – and I asked why.

"Well," she said. "My boys' warts were all gone in a week, but we were a bit disappointed for my daughter. It took hers at least ten days to go!"

I was amazed at the results – but didn't show it. I was just glad that both children were now free of warts.

The mother told me that her son was doing well at school, was involved in sports, and had many friends again.

"But I still had to take my daughter to the doctor," she said.

"Why was that?" I asked.

Evidently, I had missed touching one wart at the bottom of her daughter's back, and because I hadn't touched it, it hadn't fallen off! Hundreds of warts had, but this particular one had not. I was astounded.

"You should have brought her back to me," I exclaimed. "I would have seen her again."

The mother looked at me pityingly, then reminded me patiently that she'd been there and had seen me use up all the magic in the envelope for warts. She knew there was no point in returning because it was all gone! So, she had taken her daughter to have the last wart burnt off at the doctors. It had been painful, and she had cried. The mother also told me that she had never found a single wart in either child's clothes or bedding. She asked me where the warts had gone.

"I have no idea… it's all part of the magic," I replied.

How was I feeling? I was amazed at the results. Delighted for the children, of course, incredulous that the only wart I had not touched had remained. And I was astounded that the mother had not brought her daughter back to me because she believed that the magic was finished, because she had seen the empty envelope!

I said goodbye and went in search of a much-needed coffee.

Footnote

The work done with these children was not a cure-all for all warts. It only worked for these children and these warts. It was always my job to find a solution that was tailored to match each person individually and to achieve the best outcome for them.

Sometime later, I had a very different boy with warts.

He was older, extremely intelligent, attended a private school, and played the piano. The warts were all over his fingers. They were unsightly and were affecting his confidence. He also loved playing handheld digital games (about which I knew nothing), and he was, in fact, deeply engrossed in a game while in the waiting room.

As he sat down in the chair, I got him to explain the game that he was playing. It involved zapping and destroying invading aliens from UFO's. I decided I could get him to use this talent to destroy his warts. I induced trance, and under hypnosis, he invented just the right game, a game that zapped warts!

As he lay back in the chair, his fingers and thumbs began working rapidly in the air, zapping warts on the imaginary screen he was holding. He was making laser noises and reacting with his whole body, wriggling in the chair as each wart exploded. When all the warts were zapped, the game was finally over. As he lay back exhausted, I told him his body would take as long as it took to remove the warts and that, because his body had made the warts, his body also knew how to unmake the warts. He seemed satisfied with this explanation and nodded his understanding. I brought him out of trance, and we made a follow-up appointment at his request.

He returned two weeks later with not a single wart! He wasn't even surprised at the outcome because he'd known it would work. He was just glad all the warts were gone.

He told me he'd also been able to talk to himself in a slow voice using the exact words he remembered I had used with him in our session – *sleepier, heavier, deeper and deeper* and *more and more*, and he'd found that he could put himself into a state of hypnosis! He told me he'd used the same game he'd invented for his warts, but this time he'd zapped the verruca's on his feet! He'd caught verruca's from the public swimming pool and, despite having painful repeat treatments, had never been able to get rid of them. Now, two weeks later, they were also completely gone! Where was this going to end? I asked myself.

I explained to him how hypnosis could only be used on himself for good, for health, learning, sport, and music. I warned him that it should never be used on anyone else, as it could be dangerous. He nodded and agreed. I sometimes wonder what became of this boy – with that kind of intelligence, imagination, and focus, I am sure he would have gone on to do great things.

5

TO HAVE AND HAVE NOT

A well-dressed man arrived to see me at my private practice. He was friendly, polite and interested in what I could do. I wanted to know why he was here and what he hoped I could do for him.

He began by telling me that his life was good. He had married his childhood sweetheart and they now had two teenage children. The children were a joy to them both, did well at school, and had great friends. As a family, they enjoyed wonderful holidays together.

He talked about his job, which he was passionate about and thoroughly enjoyed. He was a manager of an Electrical Engineering company and had a good supportive team to work with.

So, I asked him, "Why have you come to see me? Your life seems good."

"It is," he replied. "But I am just not happy, and my wife has told me that I have to come to see you, to sort myself out." He explained that his wife had a friend, whom I had recently seen for successful therapy, and his wife was hopeful that I would be able to help him too.

"My wife says that I get sad and go 'inside myself.' It's true and it gets worse just before Christmas every year. Luckily there is so much happening at Christmas time, that I can just about keep going for the family's sake, but my wife still notices, and she is worried about me."

"How do you know that you are not happy?" I asked.

"It's not a thought," – he had worked that out – "It's an overwhelming feeling of great sadness, that comes from deep inside."

"Whereabouts deep inside is it?"

He put his hands over his middle – "There," he said.

"And when it's there, what's it like, when it's there?"

"A huge black empty cave," he replied.

"What does 'huge black empty cave' want to do and what does 'huge black empty cave' want to have happen?"

"It wants to keep turning the black into echoes that keep coming back to me."

I had asked him all the questions I could, and he had been open and honest with me, but we were still no nearer to understanding why he retreated inside himself, and why he became overwhelmed by this extremely debilitating seasonal sadness. I explained how hypnosis could help him find an answer from within his unconscious mind and help find a reason for his seasonal sadness that his rational mind was unable to provide. I explained that sometimes just by knowing the reason, profound positive changes could occur.

So, he agreed to be hypnotised.

He went very quickly into deep trance.

When I asked him about "dark cave," tears started pouring down his face.

"It's Christmas," he said, and his voice was that of a young boy.

I altered my voice to talk gently to the boy.

And… do you like Christmas?

"No!"

… and what is it about Christmas that you don't like?

"The presents."

… and what is it about the presents that you don't like?

"Every year mum knits me a new jumper and I choose the pattern and the colour. I help her to roll the balls of wool and I watch it grow. She measures me."

That all sounds good.

"Yes!"

And… when mum has knitted your jumper… then what happens?

"She wraps it up for Christmas and puts it away in the cupboard under the stairs."

Does anything else get put in the cupboard under the stairs?

"Yes!"

Like what?

"Lots of things like a bike, a football, roller-skates, a car, a radio, Lego, a watch."

And... where do all these things come from?

"My dad."

Do you have brothers and sisters to share these things with?

"No."

So... are all these things just for you?

"Yes!"

That sounds like a lot of things. So... tell me about your Christmas Day.

"I put on my new jumper, and I sit in front of the Christmas tree and Dad gives me the things from the cupboard and I have to unwrap all the presents carefully. Dad takes lots of photos of me with them to send to our family who live far away... but I mustn't open the boxes... and I mustn't play with the presents."

And... what happens to the presents... when you've unwrapped them... but you don't open the boxes... and you don't play with the presents?

"Dad takes them away and puts them back in the cupboard under the stairs."

What happens next?

"We have our Christmas dinner."

(At this point I am hoping this little boy is going to be allowed to play with all his Christmas presents after dinner).

Then... what happens next?

"Dad goes out drinking with his friends. Mum does the dishes. I watch TV and I am glad that Christmas is over."

And what's it like when Christmas is over, and the presents are back in the cupboard under the stairs?

"I feel sad because I never get to play with my presents. My dad takes the presents back to the shops, and he gets all his money back. But everyone thinks I'm really lucky, that I've had all the presents because he sends them the photographs. They all think he's the best dad in the world, but he's not, he just pretends to be, and it is the same every Christmas."

... And when you can't play with your presents... when you feel sad... where inside you, do you feel sad?

His hands went again to his middle.

... And when you feel sad there... what is it like?

"It is a big black empty cave. I don't like Christmas. I don't like the cupboard under the stairs, and I really don't like my dad."

(I didn't like his dad much either by this point).

What needs to happen so that you can like Christmas?

"I just want to keep a present, just one present, like I do the jumper. A ball would be all right, I could kick it on my own or with friends."

What would be the very best present you would wish for and want to keep?

He smiled.

"A train set," he said. "Like the one in the big shop window."

Wow, I agreed. *That would be a wonderful present.*

I thought I knew the kind of train that he meant – every Christmas, our local department store would create a winter wonderland in their shop windows and the best one was always the children's toy display. This featured a miniature snowy landscape through which a red and gold train pulled a long line of matching carriages crammed full of amazing toys and parcels. Children would stand outside in the snow, mesmerised, watching the train loop round and round on its tracks, until dragged away by their freezing parents.

I gave my client positive encouragements.

You will not always be a sad little boy who doesn't like Christmas, your dad, or the cupboard under the stairs. You will grow up to be a good, kind, strong man.

You will have a wonderful wife who loves you very much and children who will love you because you will always be kind and good and wise and treat them fairly.

When you are grown up you will not have to have to fear sad Christmases, unkind people or a dark cupboard under the stairs that takes away the things that bring you joy.

You will create your own real happiness for yourself and your family.

I told him that Christmas would be special and fun, and then I burst spontaneously into song and gave him a rendition of sections of 'Rudolph the Red-nosed Reindeer' and 'Jingle Bells!' He laughed out loud, and it was a child's laugh, enjoying the ridiculousness of my singing.

I told him he would feel himself getting *lighter and lighter* as I counted back slowly from seven to one. His eyes would open, and he would then be at the age that he was, when he came in to see me. He would now know that he was able to make Christmas a happy time for himself, his family, and his friends. He would be able to make the dark places disappear, he could bring light inside, and he would be happy.

His hands went back onto his middle again. He sat there like this for quite some time, and I waited quietly.

Eventually, he relaxed his hands and opened his eyes.

He said that it had been one of the most extraordinary experiences of his life. He knew that he was an adult sitting in the chair in my room, but he had heard and been astonished by the young voice coming out of his mouth. He had vividly felt again the reality of the hopeless and helpless emotions of those terrible Christmas days, that he had experienced as a young boy and which he had tried so hard to put out of his mind.

Then he said, "I am sure that's what's happening now. We buy all the gifts for the children, then my wife asks me, 'What would you like for Christmas this year?' and at that point, the light in me goes out, and I feel overwhelmed by sadness. But no more. Not anymore!"

He sat up in the chair and smiled and said, "This year when my wife asks me, I know exactly what I want for Christmas."

He left filled with optimism, like a man whose Christmases had all come at once!

Some months passed, and Christmas was approaching. The shops were full of decorations, trees and lights, carols were being played and supermarkets were selling plum puddings, mince pies and crackers. The toy display was back in the department store window featuring a magnificent train pulling toy-filled carriages through a winter wonderland. I wondered how my client was doing.

At Christmas time, many clients, past and present, would bring me flowers, cards, and gifts. There would be wine, chocolate and candles which were always appreciated and sometimes more personal gifts such as homemade jam, chutney, or Christmas cakes – all were gratefully received. These gifts were usually accompanied by lovely cards and notes. It was good to know that people had been helped over the year.

This morning, as I started opening the cards that had been left for me, a large envelope caught my attention. I opened it to reveal a handmade Christmas card that featured a photograph of my client with his wife and children. They were wearing the most outrageous matching Christmas jumpers with Rudolph on them. They were smiling at the camera, with their arms around each other, standing in front of a magnificent Christmas tree festooned with lights.

In front of them, at waist height, was spread what can only be described as a complete miniature landscape, which went from one side of the room to the other. A complex network of tracks and railway stations, complete with trains, people, villages, tunnels, roads, signals, yards, bridges, and viaducts. There were even model sheep and cows in the perfectly proportioned green fields, standing under perfectly proportioned trees. I could not believe it – it was amazing!

I opened the card. My client wrote that in the months since seeing me, he had transformed the attic from a dark unused space into his 'man cave,' creating a landscape for a model railway just like the one that he had seen in the department store and longed for so desperately, as a boy.

He wrote that his wife was very supportive of this new 'hobby' and that the children enjoyed it too, helping him make and paint scenery for the landscape. Being an engineer, he had installed switching lines and dimmer switches so that his trains could even run at 'night', while the villages, streetlights and stations lit up. It gave him so much pleasure. He said the trains were a gift from him to his younger self and he felt that he could now be his own therapist. (I felt sure that he could!).

He thanked me again in his card and let me know that he no longer suffered the seasonal sadness. He wished me and my family a Merry Christmas!

6

THE SECRET OF HAPPINESS

This time, it was a lady who wasn't happy.

She arrived for her initial consultation at my private practice. She was in her forties, well-spoken, well-dressed, and extremely unhappy, and extremely fed up with being fed up and unhappy.

There had been two failed marriages, both husbands had been good men, but she hadn't been happy in either marriage.

She married her first husband when very young so as not to feel alone. He was a nice man, but he couldn't cope with her constant feelings of unhappiness, and they divorced without having children.

Her second husband had been very different from her first. He was foreign, charming, had an interesting high-powered job, was extremely wealthy, and they lived in comfort. He spoke perfect English but when they moved abroad, she couldn't speak or understand the language and had been unable to learn it, so she wasn't able to socialise with his friends and family. Her second husband had been more interested in his work, networking, and social life than in his needy wife. His family had never approved of the marriage and once again, she felt lonely, isolated, and unhappy, and as though she was "walking on eggshells all the time." They had no children and they soon divorced – she had returned to England, still unhappy.

I asked her what she had done to try to stop feeling this way.

My client told me she had joined every kind of Church but had not found happiness in religion or the religious community, and felt worse surrounded by positive, happy people, still unable to find happiness herself. There had also been many appointments with doctors, councillors, and various therapists over the years, yet there still wasn't a solution to her problem, and happiness continued to elude her.

Medication had been prescribed, but this had not helped her. I asked if she drank or smoked, she told me she tried both for a while, more to be social and in an effort to fit in but did neither now. She felt as though other people held the secret about how to be happy but were not able or willing to share this knowledge with her.

She lived alone in a very nice house in a village near a beautiful lake. There were lots of coffee shops, art galleries, craft centres and restaurants. Everyone was very friendly, yet my client told me she still didn't have any friends, but saw that other people did, which made her feel more excluded and even sadder. Her divorces had left her well provided for with no need to work but she kept busy volunteering in charity shops.

My client said her feelings were easier to cope with in summer than in winter, because the winter was wet and cold, and the early dark nights meant she was alone at home, surrounded by her own sadness.

I asked if there was anyone special in her life?

There was a male friend in the village who was very kind. He lived in his own house, and they would visit each other, socialise and go out for meals or watch a movie together. But at the end of the evening, each would return to their respective homes alone.

I asked if she went looking for happiness, or was she just waiting, hoping for happiness to find her?

"I feel I have tried both these things, I've actively tried to find happiness and I've sat back and waited for happiness to find me, but it never has."

"How would you know if you found happiness?" I asked.

"I would know I had found happiness, because then I would stop feeling the way I do now. I do not want to keep on living like this, I am unhappy every single day.".

"How long have you felt unhappy for?" I asked.

"Forever."

"Forever is a very long time," I said.

Then I asked, "What was your first memory of not being happy?"

She described her childhood.

Her father was a stern, emotionally distant man who shouted, who was away a lot of the time. Her mother had been cold and uncaring and looking back, she felt her mother could have suffered from mental health problems. Even when her mother smiled, it never reached her eyes. My client wondered now if her father had stayed away so often because of her mother's behaviour. My client had been an only child, she remembered being fed, washed, dressed, and well provided for, but she was always alone and lonely. Her mother never cuddled her, played with her, or read to her. It was not a happy home. There was no extended family, no friends, no pets and there was no happiness for anyone.

She started to cry and told me she wanted to tell me something, but I would have to promise not to tell anyone else.

I told her that if the information might mean that she, or someone else, were in danger then I would have to act on the information.

"It's nothing like that," she said. "It's just something that I am deeply ashamed of."

I waited, listening, wondering what I was going to hear.

"When it's dark and I'm alone, especially around Christmas time, I can't bear to be inside on my own with my unhappiness. I put on my raincoat and walking shoes. Then I lock my door and go out into the village. I walk for hours and hours and, because it's Christmas, people have their Christmas trees in their front room windows. This means their curtains are not drawn, and I can stand outside in the dark and look into their houses without being seen – and I do.

"I look at people watching TV, eating dinner, washing up or cuddling on the sofa in front of the fire. All these people look content and happy. The houses look warm and happy inside. I feel cold, unhappy, and totally alone standing outside.

"I know the village well now from watching. I know who goes out to the corner shop, who picks up the children and at what times, and who walks their dog, where and at what times. I've watched and been amazed that so many people lock their doors, then just leave their keys under mats or inside flowerpots. It is a small village and people are very trusting, everyone knows everyone.

"When I know that a person from a 'happy house' has gone out, I walk up their path and take their key from wherever it's hidden, I open the door, and go inside. I breathe in the air of their house, as though I could breathe in their happiness, I want it so badly. I walk around breathing in and listening carefully for sounds of anyone coming back. My heart pounds in my chest. I know it's wrong, but I can't help myself. I've been into other people's homes like this dozens of times and it's terrifying, but I've never been caught. Can you imagine the scandal in the village if I was?"

She paused and looked down; this next bit was even more difficult to tell me.

"Next," she said. "Next… I take something."

"What kind of something?" I asked.

"It doesn't matter what the something is," she replied.

"I never take anything that I think is valuable. I just need to take something – something that will fit in my pocket. I have taken a salt cellar, but I didn't take the pepper. I have taken a Christmas bauble from a tree, a wooden spoon from the kitchen, a box of tissues and even a Christmas paper serviette. I am careful not to move anything else. I take something small, then I leave, lock the door, put the key back where I found it and walk back home.

"I keep the things I've taken for a while; I always hope that some of the happiness from the home will come with these things into my home, but it never does. I am disgusted with myself and appalled at my behaviour. I know it is not right and that makes me even sadder, and then I feel even worse about myself."

She looked down again, then continued.

"When I have too many things, I use them, like the spoon or the tissues. Other things I get rid of after a while, by taking them to a charity shop in another town. I am terrified that one day I will be caught with someone else's possessions."

My client was trembling from the effort of confessing. I thanked her for being so honest and for sharing those personal details with me. I told her I was sure I could help her. I gave her a relaxation CD to play, that held positive suggestions for change, and I made an appointment to see her again the following week.

My client never came back – I did not follow it up, I knew she had been embarrassed and ashamed by what she'd divulged. I hoped she was okay and that she would contact me again in the future if and when she felt ready.

Sometime later I saw her by chance at the shops. We recognised each other and she came over and apologised for not getting back to me, saying she kept meaning to ring me but never had. She asked if we could go and get a coffee. I agreed.

Since I had last seen her, she had got married to the man she'd been seeing previously. I congratulated her. They had sold both their homes and bought a new joint home together on a large piece of land. They agreed before they got married that if it didn't work out, then the property would be sold, and they would each get back what they put in, any profit would be split equally, this had been drawn up by a solicitor.

Her husband liked gardening and they grew all their own vegetables. He also liked building things, so he made a chicken coop, and they kept chickens. He planned to get sheep and geese the following year. My ex-client felt quite sad for the chickens, she thought they had a miserable life, so she'd got her husband to build them a deluxe chicken coop. It was shaped like a Swiss chalet, it had shutters and a painted stable door to keep the foxes out, and window boxes with yellow marigolds growing in them. There were even yellow and white gingham curtains in the windows! All the chickens had names and were very tame and would run towards her clucking to be fed or petted, whenever they saw her. Collecting their eggs made her happier than she had ever been!

Together they transformed their new home, she felt like a happy child with a new playhouse, it gave her such joy and purpose. Every room was newly decorated and there were teddy bears and dolls and stuffed toy animals with little chairs for them all to sit on. She no longer felt compelled to go out at night in search of happiness, happiness was now to be found within her own home. She had felt such relief at being able to tell me about her behaviour without being judged, that she had never felt the need to go out at night and do it again.

If the old unhappiness ever crept back she would play the CD I gave her and would fall asleep listening to it. Evidently she never managed to hear or remember the words, but she always woke up after a deep sleep feeling much better!

That was good enough for her, and that was good enough for me!

Footnote

I have no idea how this third marriage progressed. I do hope her new husband was a patient man because I felt she had found a way to begin her own healing. She had chickens to cuddle and spoil, lambs and geese to look forward to the following year and a new home decorated like a child's dolls house filled with bears, stuffed toys and dolls. She was making her own happiness and healing her unloved inner child in her own way. I would have liked to discuss the marriage with her, but I didn't – it was not the right time, but I hoped they could be happy and fulfilled as a couple.

After I left her that day, my mind went to those poor confused people who would never be able to account for the lost salt cellar, the Christmas bauble, or the wooden spoon! I do hope no one else got the blame. Then my mind shifted to the chickens, I don't think any of them would ever have the misfortune of ending up in the cooking pot!

I had not charged my client for the initial consultation or the CD – she was supposed to return for her appointment the following week. I hadn't even hypnotised her, yet the relief she felt from confessing her behaviour to me and from listening to the CD of positive suggestions for change, had been enough to allow her to start on her own successful journey to self-healing.

A couple of times a year I would arrive at work to find a basket, lined with yellow and white gingham, had been left at reception for me, containing the most beautiful speckled fresh eggs.

I knew exactly who and where they had come from – happy eggs from happy chickens from a happy lady!

7

THAT'S CLASSIFIED

I wasn't quite sure what to make of my next client.

He was tall, in his thirties, wore a designer tracksuit and looked tanned and super fit. His energy was palpable in the room – like electricity, and he was agitated and sweating. He was obviously well out of his comfort zone. It was immediately apparent to me that he would find it extremely difficult to show any vulnerability or be able to open up and talk to me, to discuss whatever it was that he needed help with. Still, he was here, so I let him talk.

My client had been in the army, but he now owned a successful business, which meant that he could not see me during normal office hours, so I had agreed to give him an appointment later in the evening to accommodate him. He arrived just as the receptionist and other therapists were leaving.

This new client had been married but was now divorced, and he had a young son. He had a great set of mates, a good social life, played golf, worked out in the gym, had wonderful holidays abroad, and owned a boat. All of this was related to me factually, without emotion. I let him continue until, finally, he revealed that although he had always enjoyed a very active sex life, now his body had completely shut down, and he was impotent.

I asked if he had seen a doctor about this.

He said no, he hadn't felt able to.

So, I asked what he'd done about it.

"I've gone out with many different beautiful women. I have paid for sex. I have tried watching porn and masturbating, but nothing has worked. I am very frustrated, and I just want things to go back to the way they were."

I wondered about his marriage and subsequent divorce and waited to see if he would bring this up… he didn't.

I explained how hypnosis worked and how the unconscious mind holds the answers that the conscious mind is sometimes unable or unwilling to provide. I told him that his unconscious mind also knew exactly what needed to happen to find a solution to the problem and make things right. He readily agreed to be hypnotised. It was probably an easier option for him than sitting in a room with a strange lady discussing his dysfunction.

I gave suggestions for relaxation and induced trance. I was surprised when he immediately went under to a very deep level and began sweating profusely. Suddenly he sat bolt upright in the chair, then abruptly hunched forward, and his head started moving constantly from left to right. His eyes were wide open, but he was looking right through me. He was seeing something else.

"Get down… shh – over there! How many? Mike! Mike!" he whispered urgently.

I turned and placed a cassette into the player and started to record. I was still taking written notes, but I thought that anything captured on the recording might prove useful for us to work with after he had come out of trance. Very often, in a situation like this, the client, although totally immersed in the reality of the experience while hypnotised, will often have no recollection of what occurred during the session. Hearing their own voice recount details can be a very powerful tool that helps to validate the authenticity of the session in their mind.

My client looked very stressed. He kept asking invisible people around him for their "position" and if they could see "anything". He appeared to be in a combat situation. It was very real to him. He was reliving it, and it seemed to be a very tense and dangerous situation. Sweat was pouring down his face, he was on high alert, and his eyes were open, frantic and darting everywhere.

I wondered who I was in this scenario. Was I on his side? Was I the enemy? Was I in any danger?

I was aware that there had been some recent cases in the news of men in America and France who had killed their wives or partners while claiming to be sleepwalking. As my client relived what was obviously a dangerous combat situation, I wondered if it was possible for me to be attacked, injured, or even killed while my client was in this heightened state. I was extremely concerned, especially as I remembered that I was alone with my client. Everyone else from the building had gone home.

My client was still in the chair in a hyper-vigilant state, looking around, when suddenly he changed position and demeanour, and he looked down. He started shouting out his full name, rank, and a series of numbers, which he kept repeating.

I wrote these numbers down in my notes, as I thought they could be important, even though they would also be captured on the recording – which we could later listen to together. I knew that the numbers would have relevance for him, although they meant nothing to me.

When I'm in a session with a client, it's not always necessary for me to know specific names, places, dates, times, or people. It's enough that the client knows these things and understands why these people, places or events are relevant to whatever answer they are seeking. Accordingly, my role is not that of an inquisitor but rather that of an enabler or a guide. I ask open, leading questions which allow the client's own unconscious mind to find the right solution to the problem themselves. The results and outcomes are so much more effective and powerful this way.

My client looked stressed and exhausted, so I spoke to him calmly and moved him forward in time, for his own protection and possibly mine, to a different moment after this event.

I asked him: *So, ... what happens next?*

He broke out in a fresh sweat that I can only describe as a tropical fever. His tracksuit darkened and became soaked through in patches. He started shaking uncontrollably, teeth chattering, and even the chair he was sitting in was moving.

Where are you now?

He said, 'I'm in the hospital."

And you are in the hospital?

"I am as weak as a kitten."

And how long are you as weak as a kitten for?
"A long time."
After a long time… then what happens?
"I get better."
And when you get better… what happens next?
"I get married."

He told me he had married the girlfriend he had been with before he went into the army. He was still very weak physically, but they had been happy and financially secure. They bought a house together, and they had a good life. When she got pregnant and had their son, he had been unprepared for the change the baby made to their lives. He still wanted to live life to the full, he craved excitement and adventure, and he wanted to take risks. He felt suffocated by domestic life.

He told me that he had bought his dream sports car, and he loved it. His car became a passport to a new rich, and exciting world. Beautiful women were drawn to his car and, by default, to him, and he succumbed to the temptation.

His wife was left at home with the baby, but his business flourished, and he often travelled away, which gave him further opportunities to be unfaithful. One affair led to another, nothing serious, no strings attached, just good sex whenever and wherever he needed it.

He took more and more risks. The greater the risk, the greater the thrill. One day, believing that his wife and son would be away visiting her parents, he brought a woman back to the house and had sex with her in their marital bed. Unfortunately for him, his wife returned early. As she came through the front door, he and the woman had made their escape, climbing naked from a back window, carrying their clothes and shoes, and laughing as they drove away in his sports car.

His wife had previously suspected his infidelity, but this had been the final straw – and now she had evidence. Her family supported her with good lawyers and helped her get a quick divorce – my client had no choice but to agree to it.

The divorce cost him a lot of money, and it nearly cost him his business. To remain solvent, he was forced to sell his prized sports car.

What was that like... when you had to sell your car?

He broke down and started to sob.

"That car was me – I was that car... she... castrated me!"

I brought him away from this memory to a time when sex was good and fulfilling when he was confident, masculine, fit and strong.

He stopped sobbing. His mood changed. There were no words, but he started moving and grunting in the chair, and his hands reached down towards the dysfunctional area in his tracksuit pants. The intensity of movement increased. I was in a predicament. I wanted his body to work, but my expectation had been that this would occur later, in the privacy of his own home. I really did not want to be present with my client when this happened, and everything started working again!

I put my notes down and grabbed a box of tissues, but I was too late. There was a spasm, the chair shook, and he roared. It was all over! His eyes flew open, his trance broken by the force of his orgasm. Angrily he stood up and loomed over me.

"What have you done to me?" he demanded.

I thought that was a bit unfair!

I was still sitting stunned, clutching the box of tissues.

I was at a loss. I had to get through to him quickly somehow. I could feel the situation escalating out of control, and I was there on my own with no witnesses or support.

I reached for my notes and quickly read to him the numbers he had recited earlier.

He froze, then glared at me.

"You can't possibly know that. It's classified!"

"This is what you said to me during trance," I said.

He sat back down, stunned.

He told me that he had been on a mission with the army, and he had caught malaria on the mission and had been extremely ill. I believed him. I had lived in the tropics and knew that he was manifesting the memory of the symptoms of malaria in my chair under trance.

He stared at me, then told me very deliberately, "No one can ever know about this mission."

I deliberately tore the notes of his session from my notebook and passed them to him. I ejected the cassette from the deck and gave that to him too.

"There are no other copies," I said. "These are yours – take them. You have everything now."

He took them and stood, looking down at me, then spun and left abruptly without a word. I heard his footsteps in the corridor before the door opened and slammed shut. He had left without paying for the session. He probably had other things on his mind.

I sat there with my heart pounding. I made sure, after this, that I was never alone with a client on my own in the building again – you just never know what or who is going to emerge under hypnosis.

A few days later, there was a note and cash in an envelope posted through the letterbox for me. My client paid for the session, and he paid considerably more. He wrote that he still did not understand how it had happened, but he wanted me to know that he was completely cured.

I wondered what would happen next, but I was sure my client was back in control of all aspects of his life. He wrote that he'd listened to the tape and been astounded, he'd remembered nothing of the session. He wrote that he'd destroyed the tape – that information was classified.

Footnote

When I saw my client that evening, I was not expecting him to experience so instantly the depth of trance that he entered. Normally it would require several sessions of us working together to achieve such deep trance.

In hindsight, I now wonder if this had occurred because he had been hypnotised previously but had no recollection of it happening.

In the same way, he had no recollection of what had transpired during his session with me, only the proof of it afterwards, when he listened to his own voice on the cassette.

There were rumours circulating at this time that the Soviets, Americans, and British were experimenting with using hypnosis in a military capacity with certain elite troops. A well-known American therapist whose workshops I later attended spoke of several cases he had personally worked on, which had used hypnosis for secret missions with Special Forces. I wondered if my client might have been involved in one of those clandestine operations.

He was adamant that no one could ever know of this classified mission. The only thing I could do was to give him all the evidence that I had collected in the session, the notes and the cassette. I also wondered if, had my notes and questions been more invasive; had I extracted the information of the country, the place, and the mission from him while he was in trance, would my life have been in jeopardy? Fortunately, I did not work in this way, no information apart from his name, rank and numbers was given, and his mission was not compromised. I believe that kept me safe.

There is a movie, 'The men who stare at Goats' which is loosely based on an actual Parapsychology Program that was funded by American Congress in the 1970's and 1980's. This program experimented with the establishment of a 'Psychic Spy Unit,' utilising 'New Age' philosophy in an effort to enhance US military intelligence gathering capabilities.

Philip K. Dick the author wrote 'Minority Report,' In 1954 set in Washington in 2054, where police are aided by psychics or precogs to predict crimes and allow the police to make arrests before they're committed. In 2022, his book was made into a film starring Tom Cruise.

Hollywood has made millions of dollars exploring and exploiting the themes of false memories, implanted memories or brainwashing and split personalities. There are also political thriller and espionage movies such as 'Sleeper' or the 'Bourne Identity,' and 'The Manchurian Candidate' where the son of a prominent political family is brainwashed with hypnosis, to become an unwitting assassin for the Communists.

If the Military has/is using hypnosis as a tool to mentally train and condition soldiers, who are not even aware that this is occurring, then apart from being ethically questionable, the ramifications are incredibly disturbing and far-reaching. Sometimes fact is stranger than fiction, and life does imitate art.

8

PREVENT THE EVENT

During my time as a therapist, I saw several other ex-servicemen as clients.

They had returned home from war very changed from the men who had left their families. There were often problems with violence, drug addiction and alcohol abuse. Some men had nightmares and woke up horrified to find themselves strangling their wives. Many had been in and out of institutions or prisons. There were huge personality changes, every man had a different story to tell, and there was no one therapy solution that fixed all.

Relationships were broken, marriages fell apart, and children grew up without their fathers. There was homelessness, anger, and despair. Some servicemen were lucky. They received help and were saved, but far too many others were let down by the system and fell through the cracks. The army did not provide the care that was needed when it was needed to those who needed it most. I think today there is more awareness of the need to reach out for help too, but in those days, there was a lot of stigma. Asking for help was very much frowned on or could be perceived as a weakness. As a consequence, many brave men who had stepped up and fought for their country came home and suffered in silence as their lives spiralled hopelessly out of control.

Some ex-servicemen did receive help. Their alcoholism was treated, they had rehab for drug addiction, they detoxed, they attended anger management classes, and they received medication to help them sleep. However, these were just stop-gap measures while the cause of the addictions and behaviours remained untreated and unresolved underneath. The alcohol abuse, drug taking, sleep deficiency and anger were not the problem. They were the manifestation of the untreated problem. It was not the enemy that destroyed them. It was the war and the orders they had carried out. What they had been required to do, what they had made happen. The things that they had seen which they couldn't unsee, and the things they had done which they couldn't undo. They had lost themselves, and they needed to be found again.

Some servicemen were lucky. They got help straight away and were able to reclaim their lives and families. For others, it took a lifetime. Some servicemen never found help, and the tragic suicide statistics tell all.

This ex-soldier had come to me as he was too terrified to sleep. He had a recurring nightmare of an actual military mission he had been a part of in the Middle East when his unit had been ordered to go into a village that they believed was harbouring the enemy. As they entered the village, women, children, and old people came out of their homes. These villagers were unarmed and terrified. The soldiers were ordered to fire at the women, children and old people. So, they did, maiming and killing. Then amongst that horror, the concealed enemy soldiers came swarming out of the houses, and it became a bloodbath of kill or be killed.

My client was visibly upset and shaking as he recounted the traumatic event. I was horrified listening to his narrative and cried for those villagers and for my client faced with such an impossible situation.

We all know that atrocities occur in war, but rarely are we confronted with the horror of the reality. He apologised for upsetting me but said he felt relieved confiding in me, as he had never felt safe enough before to be able to share the awful details of what had happened. He'd also been worried that he would be judged for his actions and for his weakness in not coping. I explained that what he'd told me was so awful that it was deserving of my tears. I made no judgement, and I acknowledged it had taken courage for him to share his experience with me.

My client was a young man with a wife and small children when he joined the army. What he'd been required to do under orders was so utterly repugnant to him that in his vivid dreams, at the exact moment he knew that the order to open fire on the unarmed villagers would come... he would automatically wake up. Again, and again and again. Always at the same point in this recurring nightmare, it was always exactly the same. So, he drank, he used drugs, and he tried not to sleep, anything to stop the never-ending nightmare from happening.

He was desperately trying to prevent the event.

My client was exhausted, anxious, sleep deprived, and consumed by overwhelming guilt and self-revulsion. His wife and family were suffering, but he was unable to be any other way, unable to explain to them the horror of what he had done and seen and how it had affected him.

"How amazing you are," I said. "And how clever to wake yourself up at that exact moment."

He looked confused.

I explained that I would be able to help him become the man he used to be. The man who loved his family and was happy to be home, who had good friends, who enjoyed sport, who made plans, who enjoyed healthy, peaceful sleep and who looked forward to the future.

I explained how hypnosis worked, and he listened with interest and hope. He calmed down and agreed to proceed with the therapy. I induced trance, and he was soon deeply relaxed.

And when you were in the army... did you have to eat when you were told to eat?

"Yes."

March... when you were told to march?

"Yes."

Sleep... when you were told to sleep?

"Yes."

Fight... when you were told to fight?

"Yes."

Kill... when you were told to kill?

"Yes," he nodded his head.

Did you follow orders?

"Yes."

Were you a good soldier?

"Yes."

Well, now your body and mind know they are no longer in the army.

You are no longer a soldier.

You do not wear the uniform. You do not eat, march, or sleep on demand.

He nodded.

And... you certainly do not have to fight or kill on demand.

You do not have to obey such orders from anyone anymore.

Who gave you the order to fire?

He spoke the name of his commanding officer, "he gave the order to fire."

And where did that order come from?

"Higher up. He was ordered to order."

You were ordered, and you obeyed.

You did your duty, and you were a good soldier, but now you are no longer a soldier.

The real you, the kind and caring you, can now hand back all of that, all that the army gave you. Your time there is served. It belongs to them. It is theirs, not yours.

You do not have to dream that dream. It is their dream, not yours.

It is their nightmare, not yours. It does not belong to you anymore.

Give it back.

He nodded again.

I gave my client time to sit in the chair with his eyes closed.

His eyes were moving rapidly behind closed lids (REM).

I continued.

It is time for you to change that which needs to be changed.

It is time for you to give up what needs to be given up.

It is time for you to dare to dream of what you want to dream.

It is time for you to make plans for your future, and your family.

It is time to think of your own deep, peaceful sleep, free from nightmares.

... And as your mind and body know how to do this,

and all the difference that difference makes,

in a way that is just right for you.
Then, and only then,
 your eyes will open safe, into the here and now.

It took him about ten minutes of sitting in silence before he finally opened his eyes.

He smiled at me, and he said that now he knew what he had to do. He was going home to talk to his wife. He said that now he really knew that his war was over.

Such a brave man.

I never heard from him again, but I did get several other ex-military men who came to me for therapy because they had met this soldier and heard his story of recovery.

They, too, wanted to find a way out of their own nightmares, a way to prevent the event.

9

THE MAN WITH THE CLAW

It happens sometimes, but rarely, thank goodness, that a client would arrive with such overpowering body odour, that I wanted to gag and not take another breath throughout the session. Furthermore, the next client into the room would also have to endure the smell. I would open windows, even in the middle of winter, when snow was thick on the ground, putting the heaters on full blast, desperate to get some fresh air circulating into the room. I always kept air fresheners in the room and had bowls of potpourri, but sometimes it was not enough!

This client was one such odorous man. He was in his early thirties, his hair was greasy and unkempt, and his clothes were worn and filthy. There was a distinct smell from his socks and stained trainers, which wafted up as he nervously shuffled around in front of me. He looked tired and sad, and I wasn't sure how I would be able to help him. As he sat down, I felt ashamed of being so judgemental when I realised that his right hand was non-functioning. It was drawn up into a distorted shape and curled onto his chest.

He had come about "the claw," these were his words, not mine.

I asked him if his hand had always been like this, and he replied no, only for about the last five years. Both hands and arms had been normal at birth, but his right hand and arm had started to get progressively worse very quickly in the last few years. Now he couldn't work, and he was living on benefits at home with his mother because of his "claw." He had seen doctors who were at a loss to explain his condition and were unable to help him. He'd even had an operation to try to restore the movement in his hand, but it had not helped.

I asked him some questions about his life. It was miserable. He had been an only child. His father, with whom he'd had a good relationship, had died a few years earlier, and he continued to live in the family home with his mother. My client felt that his mother had never liked him, and he'd never liked her. She was a lazy woman who drank too much and smoked heavily. She had been unkind to her husband and had always been unkind to him. Consequently, his father would come home from work, get changed, and then head straight out to drink and eat in the pub with his mates just to get away from her. When my client grew up, he also escaped his mother by going drinking with his father at the pub. It had been better at home when his father was alive, but it was unbearable now that his father was dead.

His mother did nothing and never had. She didn't go out to work, and although she was at home all day, there was no cooking, cleaning, shopping, washing, or ironing done. There was certainly no help with his homework when he was younger, no kind words, and no love. When he got home from school, she would give him money and send him out to buy chips for them both. That was their dinner. His mother always seemed to have a constant supply of cigarettes and alcohol, which he couldn't understand, because, as far as he knew, she never left the house, and never had any family or visitors around. She sat in their filthy home, chain-smoked and drank, it was a sad and stressful life. He told me he slept in a sleeping bag on a mattress on the floor. He had no blankets, sheets, or pillowcases. It was just the way it was.

His father died tragically in an accident. My client told me he'd been devastated, but his mother had never even shed a tear. She got the house, and he continued to live with her. The house would be his when his mother died. He told me that he wished his mother was dead too, then he could have the house now and live as he wanted to live. It was at this time, following his father's death, that he noticed his hand starting to clench and curl up into the "claw."

"And how would you live your life differently if your mother were dead?" I inquired.

"The house would be clean, my clothes would be clean, there would be good food and no smoking, and people could come round."

I asked him if he thought he could manage on his own to make these things happen.

He replied that he felt that he could.

I then asked him why he'd decided to let his clothes, himself, and his room get into the state he had described.

"It's not my job. She should do it," he said, referring to his mother.

"But, if your mother doesn't do it, is there any reason why you can't do it? You can look after yourself, your clothes, your home and your meals. You already know that your mother won't do these things for you because she's never done them in the past, and she's not going to start doing them now."

This was a whole new concept to him.

I asked him what he felt he would be able to do.

He said that he felt he would be able to have clean clothes, to be clean himself, and he wanted to sleep in a real bed with sheets, blankets and pillowcases instead of in his old sleeping bag on the mattress on the floor.

"What's stopping you from getting these things and doing all these things now?" I asked.

"I just never have," he replied.

"Just because you have never done something before… is not a reason to never do it now."

He agreed.

He thought and said, "Making these changes will be difficult for me."

I agreed, "You might find making these changes difficult at first, but you can take as long as you need to make the positive changes you want, and you will find that making these positive changes will be well worth the effort in the end."

He told me he wanted to get his "clawed hand" working like his other hand again. He thought it would be easier to do all the things he wanted to do if he had two hands that worked, and he wondered if hypnosis could help.

I explained to him how hypnosis worked, but first, I suggested we use an ideomotor response to see if his mind was willing to work this way and to check if it would be safe for him to do so.

Using his functioning left hand, I got him to indicate by lifting his index finger in an ideomotor response "Yes" to the questions I was going to ask.

If the answer was "No," his finger would remain still.

The answers would come directly from his unconscious mind, but I was limited to asking questions that would be answerable with a "yes" or "no" response.

I asked him if he understood.

His index finger lifted with a jerking movement and indicated, yes!

Does your right hand want to open up and move like your left hand? I asked.

No. The finger remained still.

Does your right hand believe that it would be painful if it could move?

No. The finger remained still.

Is your right hand able to open up and be used?

Yes! The finger responded.

Is it safe to open up your right hand to be used?

No.

Does your right hand believe it would be dangerous if it could move?

Yes. The finger indicated.

Does your right hand believe it would do something bad if it could move?

Yes.

While this exchange was going on, I watched in disbelief as my client's incapacitated right arm moved slowly down his chest. The hand uncurled and unclenched, becoming straight and then was finally held in a relaxed natural position on his lap, fingertips gently touching the other hand. To say I was surprised would be an understatement!

I looked at my client. He had spontaneously gone into a deep trance following the ideomotor responses. I lowered my voice and spoke gently.

... And when your hand is like this, what would your hand like to do, that is not safe?

He replied quietly, "My hand would like to go around my mother's neck, with the other hand, and slowly squeeze the life out of her."

This was not what I had expected to hear. It was extremely confronting and I sat there with my mind racing, looking for an ethical way to resolve what I was hearing. I continued speaking calmly, posing the question.

... And if your hands were to go around your mother's neck and slowly squeeze the life out of her, then what would happen next?

"She would be dead. I would go to prison, but I would still be glad because she would be dead."

Do you want to go to prison?

"No."

And you do not want to go to prison.

So ... in a way that is safe and comfortable for you... finding now that your right hand is instinctively going back to that familiar safe position it knows so well on your chest ... so that you cannot slowly squeeze the life out of your mother... and so that she won't die... and so that you won't have to go to prison...

To my relief, the right hand clenched again in his lap and slowly returned to its original position, curled up against his chest.

I took a deep breath and continued.

... And in the coming days, and in a way that is safe for you.

... You are going to find yourself caring for yourself, in a way that you have never been cared for before.

Living in a way that you have never lived before.

Making your own happiness... it's yours to make for yourself.

Your mother has chosen her path... but her path is not your path.

You can live your life as you wish it to be lived.

You can be as you want to be.

Taking the time to think about how you will make your life happier at the house that will be yours one day.

You have places to go that you have never been to – and you have kind and interesting people to meet that you have not yet met.

When you have thought about all of these things, and all the differences that all these things will make, then, and only then, your eyes will open to the here and now.

My client sat still for quite some time, and when he eventually opened his eyes, he was exhausted. He remembered his right hand moving and becoming straight, and he was excited and encouraged by the fact that he now knew it could.

"When my dad died," he said. "It was such a shock, and I was devastated. Nothing was the same without him, but my mum didn't care. She never shed a tear. Her indifference made me so mad that I wanted to strangle her. I wish she had died instead of him. I never realised that my hand was connected to this. I never put the two things together."

I asked him what he thought he might change first in his life.

He had so many ideas. The first thing he wanted to do was to take his sleeping bag and clothes to the laundrette. He was also going to get new sheets and blankets and make a real bed! He was going to use his father's old bed frame and put his mattress on it. He decided that he would also go for a walk in the park each day to breathe fresh air and get away from his mother's cigarette smoke in the house. I told him this was a really good positive start and that he might like to make a list and not be too ambitious at first – just to do one job at a time.

He came several more times to see me, but I never hypnotised him again. He told me his mother thought that he'd gone mad. He told her he had been mad for putting up with her for all these years and that she would not ruin his life any longer. She ignored him and kept on drinking and smoking.

He had mastered the laundrette, and he bought new bedding. He washed the bedroom windows; he didn't think they had ever been cleaned. He took the nicotine-covered curtains down to wash, but they disintegrated, so he got new curtains from the charity shop and the ladies there were kind and helpful. He threw away some of his old clothes and shoes and washed the clothes he wanted to keep. He hung them up.

During another appointment, he told me he had started to clean the filthy bathroom. He'd bleached the wash basin, toilet and bath. Then he'd taken his first bubble bath. It had been wonderful! He told me he had put his head under the water too! He couldn't remember ever having had a bath before.

He did not go to the chip shop for food anymore but chose to eat his evening meal at the bus station café or the pub where he had gone previously with his father. The people he met there were nice to him, and he made more friends.

My client continued living with his mother at the house, but they rarely spoke to each other. She continued to smoke and drink heavily; he still did not know where she obtained her supply, and he didn't care. He told me his mother wasn't well, she had a bad cough that kept him awake at night, but she still continued to smoke.

These follow-up appointments went on for months. He wanted to keep coming to see me, because I think he was proud of every achievement and wanted me to know each time he made progress. I told him he was being his own therapist now and that he didn't need me anymore. We agreed he could come back if he felt that he needed to, but I was happy that he was doing well and confident that his progress would continue.

A few months later, a letter was hand posted through the letterbox at work. My client let me know his mother had been taken to hospital. She had become ill while he was out and had started coughing up blood. She'd banged on the adjoining wall for the neighbour to come, who had called for an ambulance. He wrote that his mother had terminal lung cancer and would not be coming home again. She was going into a hospice. He was now on his own in the house.

About a month later, my client made an appointment and came to see me. What a change! He walked in clean and groomed, with a smart haircut wearing new clothes and shoes, with a subtle smell of aftershave. There was a spring in his step, and his eyes were alive. He smiled confidently as he reached out with his now functional right hand and shook my hand firmly in greeting! I was astounded!

We sat down, and he told me his mother had died. He had chosen not to visit her either at the hospital or in palliative care, and she'd died alone. I knew that it would be a relief for him that she had gone. The house was now his, and he was happy there. He had cleaned it from top to bottom and was enjoying simple things like watching T.V. Previously, his mother had commandeered the television, and the only time he'd been able to watch it was when sport was on down at the pub.

"When I was told my mother had died, I wasn't sad. I felt a tingling and a movement in my right hand, and after all these years, my claw opened all by itself," he said. "I couldn't believe it, and I wanted to come and tell you."

His hand, which had been rendered useless for so many years, had moved down from his chest and unclenched. It only took about ten minutes after having been that way for years! The hand was still weak but was getting stronger every day. His doctor was amazed and couldn't explain why this had happened but had been supportive and arranged physiotherapy to strengthen his hand and arm. My client told me he had applied for work and was hopeful that soon he would be earning an income again and could stop living on benefits. He was optimistic about what the future would bring.

I was pleased for him, the claw has done its job, and now that his mother had died, it was safe for him to have two working hands again.

Footnote

This was such a good lesson for me, to remind me once again to be very careful with suggestions made to clients while they were in trance. I could easily have left my client with his right-hand functioning. After all, it was what he had wanted. It was what he'd come to see me for. But what if he'd left the session with a functioning right hand and had then gone home and used it to squeeze the life out of his mother? This outcome does not bear thinking about.

It is such a responsibility to be a therapist. There are huge implications with every suggestion. I had to try to consider every eventuality, and I had to be aware of the bigger picture of life outside the therapy room and keep my client safe and, by default, his mother too.

My client had literally physically crippled himself, rendering his right hand useless, in order to prevent him from strangling his own mother. His unconscious mind had protected him by preventing him from physically being able to carry out this action. The unconscious mind kept that safeguard there until his mother was dead of natural causes. When she was safely beyond his reach, and this safeguard was no longer necessary, his unconscious mind had allowed the symptomatic hand to resolve itself in the space of ten minutes and become fully functional again.

The power of the mind over the body is incredible and should not be underestimated.

10

UNABLE TO LET GO

I knew the name of this man in the appointment book, it was familiar, but I couldn't place him. I looked him up in my records, but he was not a past client.

He arrived for his appointment. I recognised his face but was still not sure where from. I would just have to wait and see what he wanted and hope I would remember how I knew him.

He sat down and started talking. He told me he was a professional darts player.

Now I recognised him. He was famous and I had seen him on TV.

So, how could I help him?

He told me he had read an article about how hypnosis could be used to enhance sports performance. He told me he had always been very successful at darts – but he'd recently been affected by 'dartitis.'

I had never heard of 'dartitis,' and I asked him to explain it to me.

He said that when he stood and took aim, at the point at which he should release the dart towards the dartboard, his hand froze, and his fingers were unable to let the dart go.

This had happened to him recently in an important competition, and he'd suffered the humiliation of being laughed at by competitors and spectators. He told me he had left the venue as soon as he could, shaken by the episode, and was now fearful of it happening again. Fortunately, that competition had not been televised, and he hadn't seen anything published regarding his failure to throw on that occasion – but he was worried if it happened again then he wouldn't be able to compete.

He told me when he was throwing on his own or with friends, he had never been affected by dartitis. His mind was focused, and his movements flowed. They were automatic, fluid, and accurate, and he had no fear of being unable to release the dart. However, he was due to play in an important competition soon and was starting to feel very anxious. He knew that the competition would be televised, and he couldn't bear the thought of being affected by dartitis, of failing publicly, of people laughing and of having it recorded and played back. He said he was beginning to think that he should withdraw from the competition.

"And you have never experienced anything like this before that competition?" I asked.

"No, never," he replied. "I'm always very confident and focused during competitions."

"Where have you got the information about dartitis from?" I had never heard of it.

He told me it was something he had been aware of, people he knew spoke about it, but he'd never seen dartitis happen to anyone else. When it had happened to him, he had been competing in a tournament. A fellow competitor had started telling him about someone they knew who had suffered from the condition. This competitor went on to say he hoped it wouldn't affect my client's game, at which point – for the first time ever, it did!

I said I felt he had been targeted and this anxiety about the dartitis had been planted in his mind. I said I thought the other competitor had been trying to negatively affect my client's game, psychologically, to give himself an advantage and unfortunately, it had worked.

My client thought about this, shook his head then said, "But he bought me a pint! He said alcohol helped the other competitor who had been affected by the dartitis. It helped him to relax and get back into the game!"

I looked at him in exasperation. He still hadn't worked out what was happening.

"Did you used to drink alcohol when you were competing before?" I asked.

"No," he replied. "Some competitors do drink alcohol when they play, but I never had until that competition. I've been drinking a lot more since then, too, in an effort to relax and prevent the dartitis from coming back!"

I replied that I didn't think drinking alcohol would help. In fact, it would probably have the reverse effect by slowing down his reflexes and dulling his focus. I said I couldn't think of one other sport where it was recommended that drinking alcohol would enhance performance!

"Your dartitis problem is in no way related to your talent, your skills, your training, your fingers, your muscles, your brain, your eye coordination, your focus or confidence."

He looked surprised but relieved, and then he said, "But if it happened once, I'm worried it could happen again."

I said I believed he had been the victim of negative psychological suggestion. I told him in the same way words had the power to make him feel anxious, unfocused and cause him to fail, words also had the power to make him feel confident, focused, and successful.

I discussed hypnotherapy and how it worked, communicating directly with his unconscious mind. He was very keen to be treated in this way.

I induced trance. He was extremely receptive, I could see how he could have been so easily influenced and affected by the other competitor's words.

I lowered my voice and spoke slowly and calmly to his receptive unconscious mind…

When you were a baby, you couldn't walk, but as you grew older and your muscles developed, you learnt to crawl, to stand, to walk, to run and jump, to ride a bike.

As a young child, when you went to school, you had to learn the sounds of letters and learn to recognise words and make sentences and learn punctuation.

You kept doing this until, eventually, you could read and write fluently. Now you don't have to think about reading and writing. You just do it because you know how to.

All through your life, there have been things that you couldn't do - until you could.

I don't know how old you were when you first picked up a dart, but I'm sure the results were very hit-and-miss at first, but you liked throwing darts, and you practised, and you became good at it. You became so good that now you are a man, you are a professional darts player.

Today, you don't have to think about how to walk, run, read, write, or ride a bike. You are able to do all these things because you have learnt how to do them – and now you know how to do them.

In the same way today, you know how to throw your darts smoothly and accurately.

You are able to throw the darts without conscious thought because your focus is on the target, and all the training that you have done over many years allows the motor mechanics of that throw to proceed smoothly and accurately, as it should.

You don't have to think about focusing your brain, your eyes or which muscles in your hand and arm you are going to use.

You don't have to think about at which moment your fingers will release the dart so that it will travel accurately to the board because, you have already learnt how to do this.

Your body already knows how to do this, and you have done this perfectly, with focus and control, thousands, and thousands of times in your life.

Isn't it good to know that your body knows how to do this? It has learnt how to do this.

Your body has a talent for throwing darts, and you have trained that talent well.

Just take a little time to remember those very special times alone or in a friendly game or in a competition when everything seemed to flow, and it was like magic watching those darts hit the board, placed just as you wanted them to be placed.

My client sat forward in the chair, his right hand came up, and he threw invisible darts that only he could see past my head. He threw one after another, passing them from his left to his right hand until he had thrown smoothly and effortlessly three times, then he sat back in the chair smiling. He was elated.

I continued…

You are going to find that you will be much more alert and aware of people that you know, or of strangers, who try to influence you in a negative way. This could be either by direct or indirect suggestions through stories or articles or footage about other people with dartitis.

These are not your stories, these are not your problems, and these will not become your reality.

Just take a little time to remember those true feelings you experience when you throw a great dart.

You feel your body doing what it does so well, with the natural talent that you have and all the learning and training that you have done. Remember this feeling and take it with you. Expect great success and enjoy it, you deserve it.

Take with you also the absolute truth that alcohol does not help your game, and it will never help your game. Alcohol is the enemy to your excellence when competing.

So, finding yourself now returning to what you have always done, to the way you learned to play before, the way you know how to play already.

You are calm, confident, focused, talented, with skills and a body that knows how to succeed, with a body that knows how to play exceptional darts, with a body and mind that knows how to win.

Well, he was all smiles at this point.

It was my role to help him to help himself to believe that he could play as he knew he could.

… When your deep unconscious mind now knows that you are back on track to enjoy playing darts,

even in stressful situations,

even in front of huge audiences,

even in competitions with TV cameras focused on you,

and when you know that you can trust your eyes, your muscles, your fingers, your breathing, your brain, and your body, to remember all that they have learned for your success,

.. then and only then,

your eyes will open into the here and now,
and you will feel the difference and all the difference this difference makes.

It took a few minutes, I waited patiently, and then his eyes finally opened. He was quite emotional and said he did feel very different and he knew that he would be all right now.

I agreed.

I had the satisfaction two weeks later of watching him play darts on late-night TV, confidently winning the important competition he had been so fearful of.

It is the only time I have ever watched a darts competition. My children could not understand my enthusiasm for one of the competitors and my sudden deep interest in the game!

Footnote

At the time I saw this client I had never heard of dartitis. I did not play darts and did not watch dart competitions.

The internet had not been invented, and I could not quickly look up the condition. I did not know if "dartitis" was real or something that had been invented by the jealous competitor to negatively affect my client's game.

Whether dartitis was real or not was not the problem, the problem was that my client was in a heightened state of suggestibility while competing and as a consequence, had been extremely susceptible to the negative suggestion from his opponent, which had immediately and detrimentally affected him and impacted his performance. Luckily his level of high suggestibility also meant that I was able to successfully reverse this problem by using positive suggestions directly to his unconscious mind during trance.

I think it was important, too, that the dartitis had only affected him once. Had it occurred many times over many years, it might have taken much longer and many more sessions of therapy to reverse the effects.

Today it is possible to quickly Google up vast amounts of information about dartitis, which is indeed a term specific to darts, described by some as similar to the stage fright experienced by actors where they can freeze on stage and forget their lines.

There are now many examples involving well known darts players who have been affected by dartitis. My client was fortunate in that his condition was never commented on or televised and because it only happened that once, he was not known for having experienced the condition.

In 1986 five-times World Champion, Eric Bristow revealed he had the condition because he was having problems with the release of his darts. Bristow managed to make a partial recovery and even managed to regain his number one position in world rankings. Former World Champion Mark Webster was also affected by dartitis. In the 2017 Grand Slam of Darts, Berry van Peer suffered from dartitis, this was visible in his matches against Simon Whitlock, Gary Anderson and Cameron Menzies.

The Decent Darts website provides the confronting statistic that some research has shown that of those players who do develop dartitis, less than 5% will make a full recovery and play to their pre-dartitis standard. Thank goodness that neither I nor my client were aware of this statistic!

The term "the yips" is used to describe a similar condition of a movement disorder that is known to interfere with putting for golfers.

The yips can also be used as terminology for loss of control in baseball and usually manifests in pitchers as the inability to throw the baseball accurately. In cricket the term seems to be mostly applied to bowlers who have trouble releasing the ball at the end of bowling. The yips can also affect basketball players who are unable to release the ball for shots, or tennis players who suddenly start serving double faults. It can also affect snooker players, notably seven-time snooker World Champion Stephen Hendry.

In gymnastics a similar condition is known as "the twisties" which is described as a gymnasts inability to maintain body control during aerial manoeuvres with a feeling of disorientation of where the ground is.

In 2020 US gymnast Simone Biles, the most decorated gymnast in history having won seven Olympic medals and twenty-five World Championship medals was affected by the twisties during the Summer Olympics in Tokyo.

Whatever the condition is called, dartitis, the yips or the twisties, the sudden inability to perform an action which you know how to do, have done thousands of times before perfectly, and in the case of elite sportsmen and women is the source of their income, must be extremely confronting and stressful. The fact that at an elite level, these failures to perform are seen, reported on, televised, and then played back repeatedly is an even bigger stress factor to those already suffering from the condition. Thankfully there is now the acknowledgment and understanding that athletes and sports people are under immense pressure to perform, and there is professional help available.

Although I treated many other forms of dystonia over the years, I never had such a high-profile sports person come to me for treatment again. This client did not return. He did not need to and over the years, I had the pleasure of watching his career go from strength to strength.

Words have the power to both destroy and heal.
When words are both true and kind,
they can change our world.

The Buddha

11

THE MAN WHO SCREAMED WITH SEAGULLS

In my private hypnotherapy practice, I had a huge variety of people coming looking for help with a wide range of problems. Some came to find help to do things they wanted to be able to do, and some came for help to stop doing the things they didn't want to continue doing. Some came because they wanted to remember, and some came because they wanted to be able to remember, understand and then forget.

I always offered a free initial consultation to make sure that potential clients understood the therapy I offered and that I better understood their needs and expectations.

However, in my employment for the Psychology Department, the screening process was very different. There were literally hundreds of adults who had been referred through the Mental Health System from doctors, psychiatrists, and other health professionals. The referred client was then screened within our department and assessed to see if we could offer the therapy they needed, or if they could be directed towards a more appropriate channel for treatment.

If, after being assessed, the client was accepted to be seen by a psychologist, then their file would be put in a long row of filing cabinets where they would wait until it was their turn to have an appointment. At one time, there was a four-year waiting list. It was a dreadful situation for both clients and therapists. By the time the client became eligible for their first appointment, sometimes their symptoms had worsened to the point that families were destroyed, jobs had been lost, people had been incarcerated and tragically some had even taken their own lives, waiting for help that seemed never to come. There was an overall feeling of hopelessness. The therapists were exhausted and overwhelmed with the caseload, and clients were often left in limbo, feeling that no one cared. We did care, but there were not enough of us, and not enough hours in the day, to give the clients the therapy they deserved, in a timely manner.

Once a client had been discharged, I would pull out the next chronological file from the cabinet. It was only in very rare circumstances that people would be fast-tracked or jump the queue.

I went to the filing cabinet.

My next client had been referred by a psychiatrist. This client's presenting problem, I read, was that he had been picked up by the police and taken to the Psychiatric Ward, following telephone calls from concerned members of the public reporting that he had been behaving erratically and screaming at seagulls.

Well, this was a new one to me, but I sent him the appointment. I wasn't quite sure what to expect, but when my new client arrived, I found him delightful. In his forties, well-dressed, well-spoken, very polite, and extremely glad to have finally received his appointment.

I took down the usual details as required by the department, and when that was done, I sat back and said that I would be interested to hear about his relationship with seagulls.

He smiled and told me he thought that seagulls were wonderful! He told me that it must be amazing to fly like that and to feel so free. He revealed that he had always liked birds and had kept them from childhood, and still kept birds now.

I asked him why he had screamed at the seagulls. He looked confused, then told me he wasn't screaming at them. He was talking to them in their own language.

He said he always let the seagulls open the conversation. They circled and wheeled around him, and they were saying, "I see you," and he was merely being polite and responding back in their own language, "I see you too!" He said it was just the seagulls and him talking. This was all becoming a bit Dr Doolittle, but he was very rational, and matter of fact and I found myself nodding along. I have on occasion asked my own dog if she enjoyed her dinner or asked her if she wanted to go for a walk, admittedly, I was talking in English, I wasn't growling or barking, but I have often wondered, where does sanity end and insanity begin.

My client told me he had hated being in the psychiatric ward and he didn't really know what he was doing there, as it was full of very disturbed people. He didn't like the medication the psychiatrists had made him take or understand why they had been so very concerned about his communicating with seagulls. The psychiatrists had wanted to keep him there, so he had lied and convinced them he would stop talking to the seagulls, just so he could be released from the ward and go home.

I asked him, "So when did you first start talking to birds?"

An extraordinary thing happened.

My client started swinging his feet backwards and forwards, fidgeting in the chair and looking curiously all around him.

He spoke, and it was with a young boy's voice.

"I've got two budgies. I talk to them all the time, and they talk English to me, and they can sing."

My client, whom I had not yet formally hypnotised, had been triggered by my question about the birds and had slipped into an automatic regression. I was no longer talking to the middle-aged man who'd walked in for the appointment, I was talking with his much younger self.

I had been told that: "A good therapist is only as good as their next question."

This was going to be a challenge.

How old are you? I asked gently.

"Nine," he said.

And where are you?

"At home."

Is anyone else with you?

"No."

Where are they?

"At church."

Do you go to church?

"No... only the grown-ups are allowed to go to church."

So… what do you do… when the grown-ups go to church?
"I am going to get picked up in a car."
And who is going to pick you up in a car?
He gave two names.
Do you know these men?
"No… but they are from church. Mum says they will take me out in their new car."
Do you want to go out in their new car?
"Yes!"

The story continued. He was picked up in the new car. He sat in the back seat; the two men were in the front. He did not know them, and they did not talk to him. He didn't know where he was going, but it was a nice car.

Eventually, the car stopped in the middle of nowhere. The driver got out and came into the back of the car with him. To his astonishment, the man told him to take off his clothes, and then he did rude, hurtful, and dreadful things to him. He wanted to scream, but no sound came out. The man got out. Then the other man got in the back, and he hurt him too. Both men laughed. Afterwards, they told him to get dressed. He did. Then they drove him home.

His Mum and Dad were back from church. He was told to thank the men nicely. He did. Then he was told that the men would come again to take him for another nice drive the following Sunday. He went up to his room and cried unable to comprehend what had just happened. His underpants were dirty, so he washed them and hid them in his bed, hoping they would be dry by morning. He didn't want to get into trouble with his Mum.

Is there anyone you could tell about what happened to you? I asked gently.

"No," he started crying. "What would I say? No one would believe me."

I told him that I was glad he had been able to tell me. I told him that I believed him. I told him they were very bad men and that what they had done to him was very wrong, and it must have been awful for him.

He was crying freely now. He told me that it was arranged that the men would come each Sunday and take him for a ride. Mum told him he was a "lucky boy." He asked her if he could go to church with her instead of going driving with the men, but she shouted at him, and told him that he was "an ungrateful little boy."

This torture continued Sunday after Sunday.

I wondered how he'd managed to endure it.

He explained that when the men came into the back of the car, he came out of his body, leaving his body behind in the back seat with the men. He flew forward into the front seat so that just his body was left with each man in the back seat. He didn't watch what happened. He didn't feel what happened. He wanted to scream, but no sound came out. He said that he was always very sore when he got dressed afterwards.

He told me that when he was in the front of the car, he looked at the dashboard, he concentrated and he could see writing, dials, colours, mileage, screws and handles. When he tipped his head back, he could look out of the windscreen, and he could see seagulls flying. They were outside, and he wanted to be outside too, not inside with the men. The seagulls were screaming, and he was screaming in his head. They were flying free in the sky, and he wanted to be free too. So, he chose to be free and scream outside with them, rather than be present with the horror in the back of the car.

When the second man finished with his body and got back in the front of the car, he would "return" to his body, and the men would tell him to get dressed, and he did. The men would look at each other and laugh.

After the first few times, his Mum and Dad weren't there when he got dropped home, so he would let himself in with the key from under the flowerpot. His parents told him that church was going on longer these days. As he let himself into the empty house, he would go over to his budgies in the cage. He sobbed as he told them what had happened, and he took comfort in the fact that they listened to him. He talked to them, and they talked back to him. He was safe with them. He grounded himself with the birds.

Suddenly, he grew up in my chair, his voice changed, and we talked as adults. He had spontaneously left trance.

He told me he thought that this abuse had gone on for years but maybe it had just felt like it. He remembered that once he was old enough to go to secondary school, the car trips had stopped. He'd never been allowed to go to church with his parents.

He went on to tell me that he'd always done well at primary school but he didn't fit in at all at secondary school, everyone there thought he was weird. The teachers said that he didn't pay attention. He would often find himself daydreaming, but he listened, he learnt, and he was successful. He worked hard at school, and he studied well at home. He still liked birds and would go into the parks and the surrounding country on his bike and make lists of all the birds he could see.

He told me that he'd had a lot of problems with his bowels as a teenager and had gone to the hospital many times for treatment. He didn't like what they did, but he just came out of his body again and let the surgeons fix him. No one had ever asked him what had caused the internal trauma.

The session ended, and he agreed to come back at the same time the following week.

The next week came, and I went to the waiting room to collect him.

He said, "I'm leaving the little one out here in the waiting room today."

He was referring to his regressed younger self.

He continued, "He was really upset last week."

I nodded my understanding and enquired if the "little one" would be all right, waiting out there on his own. My client replied that he would.

My client stayed as an adult during this session, and his story continued to unfold. He was relieved to be able to talk about it, he had never spoken to anyone about these things before, because nobody had ever asked him the right questions.

He told me he had eventually done well at school. He got a good job, and while still very young, he married a girl he met at work. They were both too young, but he'd wanted to get away from his parents. They had two children, but his wife said that living with him was like having three children. He doted on his children, played with them and spoilt them, but he didn't communicate well with his wife, or help around the home, and they had drifted apart. He got some birds; she hated the birds and their noise and mess. The marriage ended. She kept the children, and he kept the birds.

He missed his children but was told that it was for the best that he stayed away. When he found out that his ex-wife had met someone else, he was devastated, and had a mental breakdown, which resulted in him finding comfort and release by screaming on the beach with seagulls.

This erratic behaviour, and his distress from the marriage breakdown, her betrayal and loss of his children, had resulted in him being sent to a psychiatric ward. After he was discharged, he moved away to another part of the country and got a good job. He bought a house and married again.

His second wife was very demanding, always wanting the best of everything, he felt overwhelmed and unappreciated. They had a child together who he doted on, but once again the marriage failed. His wife got fed up with him and he got more birds. He became an entertainer at children's parties at weekends. He said that he loved seeing all the happy, excited children. It was as though he was giving them the childhood that he'd never had.

Eventually this second wife threw him out of the family home and he ended up sleeping in his car for a while, parked on the seafront. He suffered another mental breakdown where he again sought comfort screaming with the seagulls. That was when the police were called, and he found himself in a psychiatric ward once more.

My client came back the following week and the story continued.

He told me he was proceeding with divorce arrangements, but this time he wanted to remain in his child's life, he wanted shared custody. This was proving difficult because of his psychiatric history, but he was determined to be a part of his child's life. He had also contacted the older children from his first marriage. They were excited and wanted to meet up with him. He had kept his birds too.

He said that he felt stronger than he'd felt for years, his job was secure, and he was energised and busy inventing something at work that the company was very excited about.

He revealed that he'd also been having disturbing dreams. They were about being a boy again and what had happened to him. He kept a pen and paper by his bed, and when he woke, would write everything down that he could remember, while it was still fresh in his mind. He could vividly remember the make of the men's car, the colour, the mileage and even the registration number.

Being with him was like being in a whirlwind. I struggled to keep up with him. There was so much going on.

I asked him if he had been talking with seagulls again.

No, he had been too busy.

He was happy living in the present and moving on from the wrongs of the past.

"And… the boy you left in the waiting room… how is he?" I enquired.

He laughed. "He grew up! He is here safe with me. We are doing this together."

Then he revealed that he'd been thinking about contacting the police about the abuse endured as a child but didn't feel strong enough to do this yet, but hoped he would be able to soon. I hoped he could. I already knew the names of the perpetrators, but I had no tangible evidence, and it had been so long ago. I didn't want my client to have to endure legal proceedings that may not have eventuated in a conviction. I felt that although he had come a long way, he was still very fragile, and I didn't want him to suffer further.

He asked to remain on my case list, but didn't feel the need to come every week. I readily agreed, even though we were supposed to discharge each client completely and move on to the next. I reassured him he could remain on my list and would always be able to contact me if he ever needed to. We shook hands, and he left.

A few months later, he didn't call me – I called him. I had a problem.

Our offices were in the middle of town, and each year the seagulls, lacking cliffs, would build nests on our flat roof, and we would watch from the office windows on the second floor as the eggs hatched. The demanding chicks were fed by their exhausted parents until finally, they grew feathers and could fly.

This Spring, one ambitious fledgling had taken a flying leap of faith and ended up in a heap of feathers in the car park below. The parents screeched and flew down to join him. He wasn't hurt. He flapped his wings and he ran, but didn't have a long enough runway or enough height or skill to become airborne. After three days of feeding him and screeching encouragement, the parent birds abandoned their chick and flew away.

Many of the young mental health workers from the building had tried to catch him (which had proved to be entertaining), but he'd evaded capture and just ran and flapped to the other end of the car park. The relevant authorities had been contacted, but we'd been told to let nature take its course, as seagulls were not endangered. It was then, with no parent birds as a deterrent, that a large ginger cat began to prowl with intent. More screeching, flapping, and running occurred, with the ginger cat in hot pursuit and frazzled mental health workers trying to catch one or the other.

My nerves were shattered. It was then I decided to ring my client.

"We have got a seagull who could use your help!"

He said he would come straight away.

He came by bus carrying a large cardboard box. It was good to see him and we went round to the car park. He didn't chase the bird, he just sat down and opened a tin of sardines. Then he 'spoke' to the seagull in its own language! When it squawked, he squawked. When it shrieked, he shrieked. When it screamed, he screamed. It was bizarre to watch - he did indeed speak with seagulls!

The bird looked at him suspiciously, with its head on one side, then slowly walked towards him. My client was by this time squawking very softly, and the bird had calmed down and was responding in a similar tone. The windows were crowded with staff waiting to see what would happen. As the bird got closer, he hand-fed it the sardines, then gently picked it up and put it, without protest, into the cardboard box. He carefully folded the lid and set off home.

I couldn't believe my eyes – we had spent days unsuccessfully trying to catch this seagull!

I phoned my client later that day. The bird was fine, sitting on his outhouse roof, flapping his wings and he had called him Sid! I sent a card with money in it for more sardines and signed it: "From Sid's dad, thank you for feeding my son!" I think I was slipping into a different reality.

A few days later he rang to tell me that it had taken Sid three days to learn to fly. Sid had left but would often reappear, hoping for more sardines.

The following year my client sent me a photo; it was of another young seagull sitting on his outhouse roof. He had called him, "Son of Sid." He'd found this seagull abandoned in the street and had brought him home too.

I sent another card with more sardine money, "Thank you for looking after my son," signed, "Sid!"

It was over a year later when he next called me. He wanted to make an appointment because he had something to tell me.

At his appointment, he looked confident and calm as I made us tea. He had continued to record his dreams and he had remembered dates, times, road names house numbers, mileage, and the surnames of the men.

He'd also gone back to his old hometown and met with his children from his first marriage. They'd had a wonderful time, and now kept in touch. He'd also met up with an elderly neighbour who had been kind to him when he was a child, she was very old now but still remembered him fondly. From her, he'd discovered that his parents had never gone to church, it had been a lie. They had, instead, been in the pub drinking. She told him his father had died and his mother was now in a nursing home. He did not go to visit her.

He told me that while he was there, he had gone to the local Police Station. He began to tell his story, but the policeman on reception stopped him and went to get another officer who worked in Child Protection. He was listened to, taken seriously and believed. The officer informed him, that the man who had driven the car was now a 'person of interest' to the police. He left the written details he'd remembered from all those years ago, and the police followed them up.

The police went to the house of the man who had driven the car. It was the same house he had lived in all his life. They knocked on the door. The man opened it and inside, sitting on the sofa watching T.V., was a young boy. The police questioned the boy, who told them he had to come here while his mum was out working. The boy was taken into another room, where he broke down and cried telling the officers that he didn't want to come here anymore, because the man hurt him. He bravely told them how the man hurt him, and his mother was immediately sent for.

The young boy also told the police about other boys who came to be 'looked after' by the man on different days. He was taken away to safety and the man was taken in for questioning. The man was subsequently arrested and placed in custody to await trial. My client was informed that the other abuser he had named was already dead.

My client had attended court every day and was able to sit through the subsequent trial and look his abuser in the eye, something he'd not been able to do as a child. He said he was sure the man knew who he was and felt that justice had finally been done, when the man was given a long sentence in prison. He'd faced his abuser as a man, not a child, and he felt empowered by the part he'd played in finally bringing his abuser to justice.

He'd found great comfort in helping those boys when there had been no one there to help him, but was still very distressed wondering how many other boys had been used, abused, and damaged over the years by the two men.

My client was my priority and I'd felt a huge responsibility to inform authorities regarding the abuse. Should I have contacted the police? I had no evidence beyond the testimony of a regressed nine-year-old boy, it had been so long ago, and he had a psychiatric history. I was also worried that they would discredit him because of our work with hypnosis and his history of mental health. I'd anguished over 'the right thing to do'. I had the names of the abusers but no dates, no details, no proof – and it was not my story to tell. We had discussed previously that my client would do something when he felt ready. I am so glad he did and that he had found the strength to finally go to the police.

My job, as I saw it, was to help the client overcome obstacles that had been in the way, and to help them to find the skills they needed, to be able to move forward in their lives, positively and with purpose.

Often, I was left with unanswered questions, and I never got to know the answers. Sometimes I got to hear the outcomes years later. I wondered about my client's parents, pretending to be at church, lying to their son when in fact, they had been drinking in the pub. Did they know what was happening to him while they drank? Could they not see how distressed he was when they returned? How could they not know they were sending their son out with sexual predators every Sunday? Were they complicit in the arrangement? It really does not bear thinking about.

This story does have a happy ending. My client maintained a close and loving relationship with all his children. He invented something wonderful at work which made him financially secure for the rest of his life and he continued to keep his beloved birds.

I wondered if he still screamed with seagulls – I hoped that maybe he didn't need to anymore.

Footnote

An out-of-body experience, also known as an OBE or a dissociative episode, is the sensation of your consciousness leaving your body.

This experience can be triggered by a near-death experience or by extreme trauma. Today we are aware of stories of people who have died on the operating table and who describe hovering above their body, watching and listening to what is happening around them, before being brought back.

I believe that there is a very real probability that my client had out-of-body experience triggered by the extreme trauma of the sexual abuse he was enduring.

It was his solution to project himself out of the back seat, to scream outside with the seagulls, rather than to be trapped silently screaming inside the car. That this little boy could dissociate from the terrible situation he found himself in and 'escape' with the seagulls, was an amazing coping mechanism for surviving something that would otherwise have been completely unbearable.

Often as a therapist, you are told things by clients that you know should be investigated by police or social services. Sometimes there is a huge dilemma about disclosure, integrity, professional boundaries, and also the wishes of the client. There is also the additional complication of the possibility that police, social services, or the judicial system may disregard any information obtained under hypnosis as 'false memories'. I wanted to enable my client to do what was necessary for him when he felt able to do so. Part of the healing process was for my client to finally have control over a situation in which he initially had none.

By saving the other boys from the paedophile, he had saved himself.

In the same way that this client survived as a child – by silently screaming with the seagulls, I have had other clients in therapy who told me they could escape abusive situations by leaving their bodies and "hiding on top of the wardrobe until he left".

Another client told me that they "went into the wallpaper to disappear," while another said. "I went into my teddy bear's eye." Thank goodness these children could escape like this, but it does mean that by blocking out all that was happening to them, they are often unable to satisfactorily answer all the questions they get asked by police, or in court, as adults. It's not that the abuse did not occur, it's just that because they dissociate, they distance themselves from the reality of the horror. This is why, in my opinion, so many victims of domestic abuse and rape often find it difficult to give a factual account of what occurred and are often not believed. In order to survive, they dissociate and escape to their place of safety. They were simply not there.

I found this can also be one of the reasons why victims of domestic abuse feel unable to leave dangerous abusive situations because they feel unable to be away from the wardrobe, the wallpaper or whatever it is that provides the sanctuary they know they need to survive.

12

A FREE LUNCH

Isn't it annoying and sometimes terribly embarrassing when you know that you know someone, but you just don't know how you know them?

It's particularly embarrassing when it also becomes apparent that they obviously know you well!

One such encounter occurred in my practice one morning when a vaguely familiar lady stormed into my premises, greeted me by name and then told me she needed hypnotising, "Right now!"

I had just come out of my room to collect my next client, who was sitting there looking very bemused by the situation, and I explained that I was sorry, but it wouldn't be possible to see her , as I was fully booked all day.

Undeterred, she then asked me if I took a lunch break. I replied that I did – I usually grabbed a sandwich and coffee. She said that would do.

"I'll bring you a sandwich and a coffee, and I'll see you at midday. It has to be today!"

She left in a rush.

I had hoped she would stay to make an appointment with my secretary, and in that way, I would get to know her name, look up her file, and perhaps have an idea of who and what I was dealing with.

She arrived back at lunchtime as arranged, with a delicious sandwich and the promised coffee. This was all very irregular. We sat down in my room. I began eating, and she began talking.

The previous day, she told me, she had proudly picked up a brand-new car, her first new car ever, and she had been on her way to school to pick up her daughter.

The car was wonderful to drive, and she had driven this road hundreds of times before. As she was proceeding along the dual carriageway, enjoying the luxury and smell of her new car, a large black car started to overtake her. There was a terrific bang and a terrible screeching sound as the black car slammed into the side of her car and then proceeded to scrape along the entire length as it overtook, completely removing her right-wing mirror in the process.

She told me she had been shocked and had struggled to control the car and remain in her lane. She had braked and pulled over and had expected the other driver to do the same. He did not! Instead, he had accelerated and driven off erratically down the road.

Incensed and shaken, this lady still had the presence of mind to notice the licence number as he drove away, but she had no pen and paper on which to jot it down. She always kept such things in her old car, but today she was in the new car. She kept repeating the letters and numbers like a mantra, over and over again, out loud. She was determined to remember it.

Her door was buckled and jammed. She had to climb over into the passenger seat to get out. She noticed other cars were following the black car and beeping their horns at the driver. Oncoming drivers were flashing their lights.

She stood there helpless, staring at the terrible mess that had been her brand-new car. It was then that another car pulled up behind her. It was a mum from school who had recognised her, and, luckily, she had a mobile phone. My client borrowed the phone and rang the school and told reception what had happened. It was arranged that the mum with the phone would pick up her daughter, with her own, and take the two girls for afternoon tea and a play date. Then my client had called the garage to come and get the ruined car. She then used the phone for a third time to call her husband.

It was at this point, after dialling all these phone numbers from memory, that she realised, to her horror, that she had completely forgotten the black car's licence number!

That night as she lay in bed, upset about the damage to her new car, shaken by the accident, and frustrated by her inability to recall the licence number, she decided that she would come to see me so that I could hypnotise her and help her to remember it!

"I came to you last year," she said. "You helped me stop smoking! It was brilliant. I've never smoked since or even thought about having a cigarette again! I just need your help now to remember this licence plate. I know it's in there!"

Finally, I knew that I had seen her to help her stop smoking, but I was still desperately trying to remember her name!

I agreed to help her, and she relaxed back into the chair.

It took me about two minutes to put her into a deep trance. I had obviously hypnotised her before, and she was receptive to my voice and words.

I did not need to put her through the crash experience. We just went forward to the time before she got out of the car – when she could still remember the licence plate clearly in her mind. She told it to me as she saw it, repeating it over and over, and I wrote it down. I got her out of the car, still feeling shaken and angry but safe, and then brought her out of trance.

She was ecstatic and recited the number back to me again.

"I knew that I knew it," she said. "I knew it was in there. Thank you!"

I gave her my jotting anyway.

I told her it probably wouldn't be a good idea to tell the police or insurance company that she had got the number through hypnosis. In my experience, the police get very suspicious of hypnosis and false memories.

The whole session had lasted no more than ten minutes. I didn't charge her, but I had enjoyed a lovely free lunch… and I still didn't know her name! She left as quickly as she had come, thanking me profusely. I hoped that everything would go well for her.

She called in again at the practice to see me the following week, but I was busy. She left a message with my secretary, letting me know that the police had already traced the black car's owner, having obtained the details from several other motorists who had also reported the dangerous driving. The car had been located in a local repair shop. It still had traces of her car paint on it, so there was no doubt that it was the same car. The details she had provided to the Police matched.

Luckily, this time my secretary had asked the lady for her name and number, and I was finally able to get her file and ring her back.

Now I knew who she was! She had totally changed her hair colour and style, and she had lost a lot of weight; she looked much younger than when I had worked with her the previous year, it must be the benefits of becoming a non-smoker! No wonder it had been so hard for me to remember her name.

She called in some weeks later, to let me know that the driver had now been charged with dangerous driving under the influence of alcohol. He was a well-known local man, a member of the golf club, and evidently, he had overindulged at lunchtime.

She was also pleased to let me know that she would be getting another brand-new car through insurance, as the other was being written off. She had been extremely lucky not to be seriously injured.

I was pleased that she had got the matter sorted. I thanked her again for bringing me an excellent lunch. I remember it even now; it was prawn mayonnaise and salad on a seeded wholemeal roll. Delicious!

I might be bad at remembering names, but there are certain things I don't forget!

13

PLEASE LEAVE YOUR NAME AND NUMBER

Most people I know look forward to going on holiday each year.

My next client was the exception.

He told me he hated going on holiday and dreaded the build up to it each year, becoming completely overwhelmed with anxiety.

He and his wife had invested in a timeshare abroad. They went for the same two weeks every year, to the same place (he told me it was beautiful), where they would meet up with the same friends, eat in the same restaurants, go to the same bars, sit on the same beach and swim in the same sea.

This all seemed very organised and stress free, so I asked why he became so anxious?

He didn't know.

"There is no reason for me to be anxious," he said. "The flight there is direct, transport to the apartment from the airport is good, we know where we are going, and I know what to expect. The apartment is gorgeous, the sea is blue, the food is fantastic, and our friends are great company. Wherever we go people are friendly and we are greeted by name in restaurants and bars, yet I still feel completely overwhelmed by anxiety, and each year I find it harder and harder to go.

"When I know that the holiday is approaching, I start getting anxious. As soon as my wife buys the tickets I get even more anxious. When she starts packing it gets worse and as the time for departure gets closer, my anxiety just keeps on increasing. It is unbearable. My wife can't understand why it's such a problem for me, she looks forward to our holiday each year but now I'm ruining it for her."

I wondered if he continued to be anxious when he got there.

"Always. I am anxious the entire time," he replied.

"But do you enjoy the holiday?" I asked.

"Never," he replied. "I only go for my wife's sake. I don't want to go, and I don't want to leave my business. She says I spoil her holiday because I won't go anywhere or do anything with her. It gets so bad that sometimes I cannot face socialising, so she ends up going out alone. I stay in the apartment and read a book but feel guilty for letting her down."

He went on to tell me that one year his anxiety had become so extreme that he had flatly refused to go. His wife had instead taken a relative for company but had been very disappointed and annoyed that he had not gone. He had been missed by their friends who expected to see him there. His wife had been so embarrassed by his absence, that she had lied and told their friends he'd been too unwell to fly. They had been very concerned and some had rung him, saying that they hoped to see him the following year, which had only made him even more anxious.

So, it was holiday time again, and he had to go. The tickets had been bought, his wife was extremely excited and looking forward to this holiday. She'd already been shopping for new clothes and had packed and repacked their suitcases. He was just going through the motions. He had arranged for cover at work, but still didn't know if he was going to be able to get on the plane, as his anxiety was so extreme.

He asked me, "Could hypnotherapy help?"

I explained how it worked and said that I could show him a technique to reduce his anxiety. He agreed to proceed.

He was a good hypnotherapy subject and was soon lying back deep in trance.

I didn't delve into why he got so anxious, there was not enough time as he was flying the next day, we only had what was left of this session. I just taught him a hand exercise which would help to control the anxiety when it appeared. He practised 'squeezing' the anxiety away down through his fingertips and releasing it. He was very relaxed and positive by the end of the session. I showed him the technique again, in the waking state, he felt that he had it mastered!

Two weeks later an extremely happy man returned to see me, just for a chat. He looked tanned and relaxed. He told me he'd had a great holiday.

I was really pleased and asked what had made the difference.

He told me he had started using the technique I'd shown him, to squeeze the anxiety away, but then he laughed and said he had found something which worked much better.

I was intrigued, I am always open and ready to learn more.

He told me that early each morning he would get up and go for a walk while it was still cool, to get coffee, fresh bread and croissants from the bakery near the apartment. His walk took him past a public telephone. He knew the UK code and had my practice number on a card in his wallet. Every morning, hours before my secretary arrived at work, he fed in his coins and rang the number.

The answer phone picked up his call and played my recorded answering machine message.

'I am sorry… I am not available to take your call right now.

Please leave your name and number and I'll get back to you as soon as I can'.

"I rang and listened to your voice every morning," he said. "When the answer machine beeped I would hang up but listening to your voice gave me a feeling of complete calm which lasted all day. After listening to you, I felt as relaxed standing in that telephone box as I did when I was hypnotised in your chair."

He had felt so relaxed and anxiety free that he'd been able to go out shopping with his wife. He had gone to markets, restaurants, bars, and cafes. He had socialised and eaten out, bravely trying foreign dishes that he'd never tried before. He swam and jet skied and even tried paragliding! He had suffered no anxiety, and his wife had been extremely happy – they had both enjoyed the best holiday ever! I was really pleased for them both.

My client brought me a beautiful earthenware fruit bowl, hand painted with large yellow lemons, and green leaves from one of the local markets, handing it over to me saying, "This is with gratitude from my wife."

After he left, I went downstairs to see my secretary. I had something I needed to tell her.

Each morning my secretary arrived before me to tidy the rooms, check the answering machine, and organise my appointments. Over the last two weeks she'd become increasingly concerned about a mystery caller who had been ringing very early at the same time every morning. This caller always hung up, leaving no message. Concerned for their well-being she had tried ringing caller ID but had not been able to retrieve a number to ring the mystery caller back.

"You know the mystery phone calls that have been troubling you for the last two weeks?" I said. "You don't need to worry, we aren't going to be getting any more of them."

And we didn't, until a year later, when I knew it was my client's two weeks of timeshare again. He once again rang our answer phone, calming and grounding himself, dealing with his anxiety, by listening to my recorded voice message!

Footnote

I never did find out why going on holiday had become such a problem to my client, it didn't make sense to him either, but he didn't need it to make sense, all he needed was a solution to his problem. By making that long distance phone call and listening to my voice on the recorded message, he regained control, and solved the problem. He could now relax with no anxiety and enjoy his holidays.

When I knew I was retiring, closing my private practice, and leaving the country, I was concerned that my client would no longer be able to listen to my answering machine message.

I therefore sent him a complimentary relaxation CD. I included a note, explaining that my voice on the CD would have the same effect for him as the recording. He contacted me and thanked me but said he'd been on holiday several times since, and he hadn't needed to be reassured by listening to my answer machine message. He told me he now looked forward to his holidays each year and no longer suffered from anxiety.

I had another interesting experience of a client being affected by my voice.

I had appeared on Television as part of an early morning show about complementary therapies and had spoken a few times, giving my opinion when asked on various issues. I was astonished to be contacted later that day by an ex-client who I had not seen for many years. She'd been at home ironing in front of the television and was surprised and interested to see her therapist on the show.

She switched off the iron and sat down to watch and listen and when I spoke she had spontaneously closed her eyes, lulled by the familiar sound of my voice. She woke up twenty minutes later as the programme ended, feeling extremely relaxed but twenty minutes behind in her ironing.

This was another lesson for me to learn. I'd always cautioned my clients to never listen to the relaxation CD's I gave them when they were driving, operating machinery or in a dangerous situation. The voice I used during hypnosis was slow, low and gentle, I had no idea until I heard from my client, the holidaymaker and this ex-client watching me on television, that my normal speaking voice could be such a powerful trigger.

14

GROUNDED BY FEAR

This next client told me she felt very fortunate: she had a wonderful husband and adult children who were doing well. They had a beautiful home, a privileged lifestyle, and were financially secure. She had travelled the world, first as a student with friends and later with her husband and family, they always took exotic or adventurous holidays. Her life sounded good, so I wondered what I could do for her.

Her husband (whom she had hoped would be thinking about retiring), had just taken on a new role as a hotel consultant, which meant he was required to travel overseas. Such was the nature of these trips that she was able to accompany him. Initially, my client had been very excited, the first trip was to Singapore, and she was looking forward to escaping the cold and the snow. A car picked them up and took them to Manchester airport. Check-in was uneventful, they were flying business class, and waited in a pleasant lounge having refreshments. Then their flight was called. It was familiar, yet exciting, and she was looking forward to time away with her husband.

It was then that it happened. As they stood and started to board, she froze, unable to move or breathe easily, her heart pounded, she felt absolute terror and thought she was going to die. Medics were called, and as her husband stood by helplessly, completely distraught, she was attached to machines and monitors. Finally, they were informed that 'it was just a panic attack'.

It didn't feel like 'just a panic attack', she'd never experienced a panic attack before but now felt such an overwhelming sense of fear that she was unable to move. The last call for their flight was announced and all the other passengers had boarded the plane. Her husband told her they had to go, but she couldn't go anywhere. She insisted he flew without her, he had to, it was his first job for the new consultancy, and he couldn't let them down. She felt upset and embarrassed, because she'd caused a lot of disruption to the other passengers and delayed the flight as her luggage had to be retrieved from the plane.

Her husband reluctantly boarded without her, and once the medics had decided it was just a panic attack she was abandoned by the airport staff to wait alone for her son to pick her up. By the time he arrived, she had calmed down, but was very weepy when rescued. She just knew with absolute certainty that if she'd got onto that plane, it would have been catastrophic, yet strangely she was able to tell her husband to fly because she didn't believe anything bad would happen to him.

The next day her husband rang from Singapore. He was still very concerned and felt guilty for having left her alone. He wanted her to go and see their doctor for a check-up. She agreed but assured him she was feeling fine. His flight had been good, the hotel was wonderful, the new job role was interesting, the restaurants and shopping were amazing, everything was perfect, apart from the fact that she wasn't there with him. He told her he would be home in a week, and promised to ring each night. He told her he loved her. She was concerned when he was flying home, but didn't panic, and didn't fear disaster.

About two months later, her husband was required to fly again, this time to Dubai. He asked if she wanted to go with him, it was a much shorter flight. She had suffered no further panic attacks but was still too afraid to even think about getting on a plane and declined. She had however been able to drive her husband to the airport and went into the terminal to wave him off, experiencing no anxiety or panic, and so, it had continued, for about three years. Now, she wanted to be able to go away with her husband again, she missed him, and missed the travel, but she feared the fear and worried that the panic would come back and wondered if hypnosis would be able to help.

"Have you spoken to your doctor about this?" I asked.

"My doctor has prescribed tranquilisers which I could take before I fly. He also suggested I see a counsellor which I have done but it didn't help. He also recommended a psychiatrist, but I didn't feel that I wanted to."

"I don't feel that these things are addressing the problem," she said. "It's strange because I can happily watch my husband get on a plane and I feel no fear. I can watch plane disaster movies with no anxiety and my daughter has recently flown with her family to Spain and I experienced no panic or distress. I have flown all over the world so many times with no problems before, I just don't know why I reacted the way I did on that day, and I cannot make sense of it but I dread ever feeling like that again. Do you think you can help me with hypnosis?"

I said I would certainly do my best.

I was interested to know why, after all those many years of happy flying all over the world, she'd suddenly had such an extreme reaction and panic attack on that day.

I hypnotised her, and she went into deep trance.

I was worried she might experience a panic attack again under hypnosis, so gave assurances that I could bring her out of the state at any time and if she felt she needed to come out of trance, then all she had to do was raise her right arm.

She agreed.

Drifting back in time, to the very first time... when you first became afraid of flying...

Her eyes moved quickly from side to side behind closed lids. Her breathing became shallow and rapid. Her hands went up to cover her mouth, and she suddenly leant forward in the chair and let out the most ear-shattering scream, followed by uncontrollable sobbing. It brought my secretary running into the room. I gave her a thumbs up, and shooed her out.

My client's head was jerking in all directions.

"No! No! No!" she shouted.

And where are you?

"Manchester."

And you are in Manchester. What is happening?

"There are hundreds and hundreds of people."

And where are these hundreds and hundreds of people from?

"From the shops and the offices."

And what are they doing?

"They are running and screaming and crying and some have fallen down in the street!" she sobbed.

And what do you do when they are running and screaming and crying and falling down in the street?

"I am frozen, I can't move," she whispered.

And for how long are you frozen, and for how long can you not move?

"I don't know."

And after your body knows how to move again... where do you move to first?

"Back to my car."

Then what do you do?

"I go home."

And when you go home, what do you do first?

"I put on the TV. It shows a plane has crashed."

And what does the reporter on the TV say?

"That Manchester United football team has been on a plane, and it has crashed and they are dead! Everyone is crying, I can't bear it, I can't watch it anymore."

Her hand moved forward, and she appeared to switch off the TV.

Her breathing slowed. She calmed down.

And, from all that you have remembered and learnt today, you will know exactly what needs to happen so that you can choose to go to an airport in the future. So that you can choose to get on a plane whenever you want to and so that you can go wherever you want to go, without the fear of experiencing fear.

The past is important, and whatever happened in the past is important, but that was then, and this is now.

You can remember as much as you need to remember... and you can forget as much as you need to forget.

She nodded.

Just take some time now to remember all the good times you had when you flew to wonderful new places as a student with your friends.

She smiled.

I gave more positive affirmations.

And just take a little time now to remember all the amazing places that you have been to with your husband and children, the happy times you had there, and the wonderful memories that you made together.

Your husband loves you, and you love him.

Think about how good it will be to be able to accompany him on his business trips and have new experiences with him. Together, you will see new sights, eat new food, and make more good memories.

She smiled and nodded.

And when you are ready, and you know that you are safe, then and only then, your eyes will open into the here and now.

She finally opened her eyes and asked for a glass of water. I gave her a drink, then she started talking.

"I think I know now why I had the panic attack," she said. "Many years ago, I was out shopping in Manchester."

She told me what she remembered about that day, the 6th of February 1958.

As my client talked I realised I knew exactly what she was talking about, because I too had seen the news reports at the time. She'd been caught up in something totally outside her comprehension on that day, finding herself standing in a crowd of people who were watching with horror as a report on black and white televisions in a shop window, brought the shocking news of a horrific plane crash at Munich Airport.

This crash had caused the death of many people, among them, eight Manchester United footballers who were held in high esteem by the people of Manchester. My client didn't watch football and she had never watched Manchester United play, but she'd been overwhelmed by the reaction of the people around her, and by the horror, shock, grief, despair, and hopelessness that had been caused by the unthinkable tragic loss of the lives of the many people aboard that plane.

My client now believed she knew what her fear and panic attack at the airport that day had been about.

But it was not what I expected.

It was not a fear or panic of flying, for either herself or her husband. It was not even a fear of dying. It was not the fear of hijack, explosion, engine failure, bombs, or crashing. Her fear was instead for her family. She wished to spare her family from ever experiencing the extreme emotion that she had experienced and witnessed on the streets of Manchester that day.

The only way in which she knew that she could prevent this from happening was by not flying. This thought process made absolute sense to her, by not flying, she was sparing her family the possibility of her future loss. She made sense out of nonsense, and then she told me why it had finally made sense to her.

On the day she suffered the panic attack at Manchester Airport, as they were getting ready to depart, all the passengers had been held back while a sports team boarded the plane first. The team was wearing matching club colours. In her mind, it had all come together, a sports team, a plane, Manchester Airport, cold weather, snow, and flying. In her mind it had triggered impending disaster and unbearable loss. Seeing the team board, sent her mind back to that terrible day in Manchester in 1958.

She hadn't ever put these two things together, because so much time had elapsed between the two events. However, she now realised that the emotions she had felt, standing with those devastated people on that fateful day, and the emotion and panic attack she experienced, triggered by the sight of the team boarding, had been exactly the same.

She was completely exhausted, and it was the end of the session.

I felt we needed another appointment, as I was concerned that I had not had enough time to fully address all the issues she had revealed. She agreed to return the following week and I told her to ring me if she needed to see me before that.

The next week my client didn't arrive for the scheduled appointment. I was not pleased as I expected people to have the courtesy to cancel if they couldn't attend, so other clients could be offered their appointment time.

Then my secretary came through and told me that my client was on the phone.

I took the call. It was a bad line, and I could hardly hear her at first.

"I apologise for missing our appointment," she said.

"Are you all right?" I asked.

"Oh yes!" she laughed. "I'm in Italy!"

I thought I had misheard, but no, she was indeed in Italy!

Her husband had gone on a short business trip to Rome and booked into a hotel they had been to together many years earlier. As always, he'd asked her to go with him, but as always, she had declined. She dropped him off at the airport as usual and as she watched him go alone into departures she thought, I want to go to Rome!

Then, she asked herself if she could do it. Feeling no apprehension she thought she could!

She went home, booked a flight, packed a bag, and drove back to the airport and parked the car. She checked in and went to the departure lounge - there was no panic.

She ordered a gin and tonic… no panic.

The flight was called… no panic.

She boarded on her own… no panic.

She landed in Rome, retrieved her luggage, and got a taxi to the hotel. She ordered coffee and waited for her husband in the lobby.

He walked in and couldn't believe his eyes. It was a very happy reunion, and a memorable week. The first thing they did was ring their family at home who were thrilled she was in Rome. Then she decided to ring me at her appointment time to apologise for missing the appointment. It was the best news.

I later received a postcard from her of the Colosseum. Postcards from this client continued, and every few months there would be another view from another far-flung place. This carried on for many years, and my secretary would pin them up on the notice board for everyone to enjoy. We all looked forward to seeing where she went to next!

Footnote

The Munich air disaster occurred on six February 1958 when British European Airways Flight 609 crashed on its third attempt to take off from a slush covered runway at Munich-Riem Airport, West Germany. The aircraft was carrying the Manchester United football team, nicknamed the 'Busby Babes' along with supporters and journalists. There were forty-four people on board, twenty of whom died at the scene, three more died later in hospital – Twenty-one survived.

15

THAT SINKING FEELING

My next client came during his lunch break.

He was happily married, had a wonderful wife and two sons – the youngest was starting university, while the eldest had recently graduated and got his dream job in marine biology. As a family they always spent the summer together, staying in the same place in Greece, a lovely villa with a pool, in a small village on the coast.

Over the years they had become friends with the owners of the villa, a retired English couple who had moved to Greece some years earlier. They returned to the UK each summer to visit their family and were happy to rent their home out to my client while they were away. The villa was maintained by a local lady and her husband looked after the house, pool, and gardens. They even brought in shopping and supplied fresh fish, fruit, and vegetables. This arrangement had lasted for many years. It was a wonderful home away from home and was fully renovated with all the mod cons, yet still managed to retain its local charm.

My client's wife was a published author and she felt she did her best work at the villa during those weeks away each year. While she wrote, my client spent time with their two boys.

He had taught both of his sons to swim in the pool. They were strong swimmers and also swam and snorkelled in the sea, diving from a small boat that came with the villa. His sons would often have friends over from the UK to stay for the summer and they also socialised with the local boys with whom they had grown up.

I'm sure my client could have kept on talking about his family and holidays, but I had to stop him and ask directly, what he had come to see me about.

He found it difficult to tell me. He was obviously a man who was used to sorting out his own problems. It took courage, but eventually, he said,

"I can't swim."

"But you have just told me that you taught both of your sons to swim?"

"Yes, because that was in the pool, and I could hold onto the side and touch the bottom with my feet."

"Both my boys learnt to swim really quickly. They were confident and competitive and as soon as they could do a few strokes they could do a width, and then full lengths of the pool. Now they both swim, snorkel, and scuba dive in the sea, but my problem is that no one in the family knows I can't swim. They just presume that I can. It didn't matter before, because when we used to go for holidays, I would fly backwards and forwards to the UK for work and so I got away with it… no one noticed I couldn't swim."

However, things were about to change.

My client had been offered early retirement from work and had also recently come into a sizeable inheritance. The villa owners in Greece told him they were planning to sell and move back to the UK, because of their age and deteriorating health. They had offered my client the opportunity to buy their villa at a very good price, including all the furniture and even the boat. The local couple wanted to continue working there, and his family were keen for them to buy it. So, he would retire, and they would be buying their dream villa.

"That's fantastic," I said.

"No," he said. "It's not, because they don't know I can't swim!"

"So, what have you done about this?" I asked.

"I booked some private swimming lessons at the local sports centre, but I simply couldn't get into the water. I had a panic attack and left – I haven't been back!"

"I'm dreading the move to Greece. The villa sale has gone through, but I don't know how to tell my family I have never been able to swim, and once we live there permanently they're going to work it out. I'm worried my wife will think I was irresponsible, I was always left in charge of the boys in the pool when she was writing, she doesn't know that I can't swim. I can't tell anyone, and I don't know why I am so afraid of the water. I feel stupid."

"Did you have swimming lessons at school that frightened you?" I asked.

"No."

"Have you ever been to the beach as a child and had a bad experience?"

"No."

"Have you ever fallen into a lake or river?"

"No." He racked his brain, but he couldn't come up with a reason to explain why he was so scared of water and unable to learn to swim.

I told him he might not know the reason for his fear, but that his body would. I told him that through hypnosis, we might be able to understand the reason and find a solution to his problem. He agreed to hypnotherapy.

As I induced trance and counted down from one to seven, he relaxed.

I lowered my voice to speak to his unconscious mind.

... And drifting back in time to the time when you first felt fear in water...

Immediately he started spluttering and gasping for breath, clawing up at the ceiling, he was literally drowning in front of me sitting in the chair.

I swiftly moved him on from this memory *to a safe and comfortable place in time.*

My client was able to breathe normally and tell me he was with his boys, laughing and playing in the shallow end of the villa pool, with his feet firmly on the bottom.

And do you feel safe in the pool?

"Yes."

I got him to take a few steps nearer to the middle of the pool, instructing him to keep his feet firmly on the bottom.

And do you still feel safe?

"Yes."

Could you choose to push off in the water and reach for the side?
"Yes."
Remember to breathe.
"Yes," he inhaled noisily through his mouth, filling his cheeks with air.

I was brought out of my pleasant reverie of imagining the warm water of the pool in the Greek sunshine, with happy boys, when my client unexpectedly started moving.

He was lying on his back, upside down, in my reclining therapist's chair, wearing a very smart business suit, when his hands went shooting out in a wide breaststroke, nearly knocking me over, while his legs started kicking furiously off the footrest!

Remember to breathe! I cautioned calmly, retrieving my glasses and notes from the floor.

He nodded and exhaled noisily through his pursed lips, kicking and swimming, face furrowed in concentration, cheeks holding in and releasing great breaths of air. He looked like a turtle flipped on its back, legs and arms paddling frantically.

Make sure you can still touch the bottom of the pool with your feet I cautioned.

He nodded as he swam, he couldn't speak as he was too busy swimming and gulping in air.

Would you like to swim a width of the pool now? I asked.

Again, he nodded.

Make sure you can always reach the edge of the pool with your arms.

He nodded, and kept on 'swimming' still breathing noisily, eyes wide open staring at the ceiling as he swam towards the edge of a pool that only he could see. As he swam he started to develop a rhythm with his arms, legs and breathing.

Would you like to swim a length of the pool now? I asked.

Again, he nodded.

I reminded him to make sure that he could always reach the side if he needed to. He nodded, and kept on swimming in the chair, concentrating hard. He knew that even when his legs couldn't reach the bottom, his hands could still reach the sides, so he was safe. For about ten minutes he swam lengths, up and down in my chair, huffing and puffing with exertion until he finally stopped frowning. He was enjoying the sensation; his arms and legs knew what to do and his breathing took care of itself.

I gave a lot of safety suggestions about pools, rivers, lakes, and the sea. I told him he would always consider his safety, and the safety of others, and he would be aware of depths, distances, tides and currents.

I finally brought him back to the edge of the pool, and safely out of trance.

He said he felt as though he had been swimming in the pool in Greece with the warm sun on his back. He was exhausted but very pleased with himself. He felt confident and thought he might go back to the sports centre for lessons. As he stood to leave, I noticed that the back of his suit looked very crumpled. I wondered what his colleagues would think when he returned to the office.

A few weeks later he invited me out to lunch at his favourite Greek restaurant.

I went.

We ordered, and then he said he had something important to tell me.

"The day after our session," he said, "I went back to the sports centre. I got into the pool at the shallow end, and I lunged to the side. I went further and further out to the middle of the pool, keeping my feet safely on the bottom, remembering to breathe, then I lifted my feet, and kicked and swam until I reached the edge!"

"Wonderful," I said.

"But that's not all! Then I swam a width, keeping near the edge of the pool. I didn't put my feet down once!"

"Then," he said, "I decided to swim a length. I kept close to the edge so I could always reach it if I needed to, but I didn't, and I swam the entire length of the pool without stopping. My arms and legs just knew what to do and I just breathed and swam. It was awesome. When I got to the deep end I got out. I couldn't believe that I had done it!"

He said he had hated the echoey noise and the smell of the chlorine and the bright artificial lighting. He showered, changed, and left the sports centre. He felt ready to swim with the Greek sun on his back, with his family, in their villa by the sea, always taking care, and always remembering to breathe.

He told me their English home had been sold and they had thrown a final party for friends and relatives before they left for Greece. At the party he'd confessed that he had never been able to swim, telling everyone he had been to see a hypnotherapist to overcome his fear of water.

His friends and family were astounded, nobody had known he was afraid of water, and no one had ever realised he couldn't swim.

Then his older sister had announced, "But it makes perfect sense that you would be afraid of water – don't you remember? You nearly drowned as a baby!"

Everyone went quiet as she told the story.

When they were much younger, they had been put in the bath together and she had been told to look after her brother. He was only a baby and had overbalanced and slipped under the surface. She desperately tried to lift his head out of the water so he could breathe but she couldn't because he was too slippery. Terrified, she had screamed for their mother, who rushed in and rescued him from under the water.

No one had ever told him this story before, but now, he finally understood why he had been so afraid of water.

"Even as an adult," he said. "I have never taken baths. I hate them. I couldn't bear the feeling of being underwater, I always have a shower instead. But now I'm looking forward to Greece, the sea views, the sun, a warm pool, and that glorious feeling of swimming through water."

Months later I received a handwritten letter from Greece, containing photos of my client and his family.

In the pictures, they were swimming in the bluest of seas and the best photo was of my client diving headfirst into the water from the deck of a large boat! He thanked me again, and wrote that he had started scuba diving, he had always wanted to be able to dive with his sons, and now he could. He was enjoying his retirement, life was good.

Footnote

I have no idea how old my client was, when he slipped under the water in the bath. He was possibly too young to even speak, as he uttered no words as he 'drowned' in my chair, but his body had held onto the frightening memory, 'water, I can't breathe… I am going to die'.

I imagine he would have continued to be put in the bath throughout his childhood, but I'm sure he would've been carefully held and supervised.

I think we need to seriously rethink sayings such as, "He is so young, he won't remember this." Trauma is always remembered in one way or another.

Trauma could be revealed or remembered through a sound, a smell, or the fast beating of a heart. It could be sweating or a sinking feeling, a heavy weight on the chest or an inexplicable fear, for example, of water.

Often, symptoms that manifest in an adult are misunderstood and misdiagnosed when sometimes they could be attributed to earlier trauma. Treating the symptoms without understanding and dealing with the cause, however long ago that cause might have been, will be unlikely to be as successful.

People that have endured and survived traumatic experiences in early childhood are usually unable to recall these experiences verbally while being unable to forget them nonverbally.

Symptoms are a solution waiting to happen. The original story needs to be told in a way that is safe. The body already knows the story, it was there, it experienced it. Allow the story to be told of the trauma that happened to the child and let the healing begin of the adult survivor.

16

MADAM MY WILLY IS NOT WORKING WELL

It was late in the day. I had seen eight clients one after another. My secretary had managed to get mugs of tea and biscuits through to me, but I was mentally drained, tired and hungry. Before leaving, she stuck her head round my door, to let me know that there was an extra booking for a free consultation at seven p.m.

I didn't usually work that late on my own, but she said the client was, "A doctor with a foreign accent who sounded nice!" He was driving through from another town after work specially to see me.

I made myself another mug of tea and waited.

The doctor arrived and it was a pleasure to meet him. He was a smartly dressed well-spoken Asian gentleman who shook my hand, apologising for being so late but said it was the only time he could get through and it was important that he saw me, as he was sure I would be able to help him.

He'd heard about me and the work I did through a colleague who had attended a dinner, where I had given a talk. The doctor had felt compelled to come. We sat down and I took his details and then I asked what it was that he thought I could help him with.

"Madam," he said formally. "My willy is not working well."

Part of me was glad the doctor wasn't going to bombard me with medical jargon that I wouldn't understand, and part of me was hoping that the 'not working' was going to be the very common problem of not being able to urinate in public toilets. I braced myself for what would come next.

He went on to tell me he had never had a problem with his 'willy' before, but now it was not 'responding'. His wife was very upset and was taking this personally, thinking he did not find her attractive any more or that he had fallen out of love with her.

I asked him to tell me more about his life and marriage.

After qualifying in medicine in Asia, he'd taken the advice of his supportive family to further his career overseas and had come on his own to the UK. It had been a difficult time when he first arrived, living alone, shopping and cooking, doing his own laundry, using a different language, and having to commute and cope with his new high-pressured hospital position. Slowly he had adjusted to the English customs, the wet weather, the language, and the food. He laughed as he told me he now knew that sprouts were not baby cabbages!

He told me he loved the challenges of his work and was enjoying being part of a team. What he needed, he decided, to make everything perfect, was a wife. Some of his overseas colleagues had met and married English women, but he wanted his wife to come from his own country and background. He had instructed his family to find him a suitable wife, and they did. The wedding was arranged, and he flew back home. On the wedding day, he'd still never met his bride, all he'd seen was a photograph of her, but he trusted in his family and in the process completely and believed they would find him the perfect wife.

At the wedding ceremony, he lifted his new wife's veil and gazed on her face for the first time. She was so beautiful it brought tears to his eyes. He told me his wife's own eyes had filled with tears because she was pleased that her face had pleased him.

His wife was very young, and she didn't speak English. He left her behind in the care of his family and came back to the UK alone to buy and prepare a house for them to live in together. Eventually she flew over to join him, chaperoned by a family member. They were extremely happy in their new married life together.

He went on to tell me they now had three teenage children who were all doing extremely well at school. They studied hard and helped each other and they, 'brought no trouble home'. They all wanted to study medicine when they left school. The children had integrated well, were ambitious and had many friends.

Their home life was very traditional. The children helped their mother shop, prepare, and cook meals. His wife never went out alone, did not speak English fluently and was nervous with strangers. She was shy and did not accompany him to work events with his friends and colleagues. They worshipped together and their lives were just as they both wished them to be. He 'honoured' her with his body, and she 'honoured' him with her body. He had only ever been intimate with his wife, but now his body had let him down, and it was upsetting them both greatly.

"Have you been examined by a doctor?" I asked.

He said he hadn't.

"Are you stressed at work, or over tired?"

"No more than usual," he replied.

I asked him to tell me what had been happening in his life around the time when the problem first began.

He became uncomfortable and embarrassed, then he told me.

He had been working late at the hospital doing administration when the door to his office opened, and a nurse entered without knocking. He recognised her from his ward. He asked how he could help, but she didn't answer, and to his amazement as she stood in front of him, she began to take off all her clothes, until finally she stood before him completely naked. He sat frozen in his chair, not knowing what to say or do.

"So, what did you do?" I asked.

"Nothing."

He then told me that the naked nurse had come around, bent over his desk next to him, and made herself available for penetration. So, like a man in a dream, he stood up, undid his trousers, and penetrated her.

"Then what happened?" I asked.

"I immediately withdrew and did up my trousers. The nurse said nothing, she stood up, got dressed and left my office, closing the door quietly behind her."

"I sat down behind my desk with my head in my hands,' he said. "I could not believe what had just happened."

"So, what did you do next?" I asked.

"I washed myself and went home," he replied.

He had been in shock. He said he didn't know how he had allowed it to happen. He could not face his wife, and he could not 'honour' her in their bed that night. He felt unclean and as though he'd destroyed their wedding vows. His wife was devastated and didn't know why he had changed towards her. He couldn't tell her; he could not tell anyone. He told me he had never seen the nurse again, but he did hear eventually that she had transferred away from the hospital, and he had been relieved she had gone.

"Well," I said. "Thank you for telling me what happened, that was a terrible situation that you found yourself in."

I asked him to go back, to remember the time when he first came to England. What had he found strange, what had he found different or difficult from the way things were in his country?

He told me he had mistakenly shaken sugar all over his dinner because he thought it was salt, and people had laughed at him. He said that initially, he knew he looked different to his colleagues because, although the clothes his parents had bought him to wear were smart, they were traditional and did not look right in the UK. He became aware of these differences and, he made changes and westernised his appearance. He bought suits, and he had his hair professionally cut. He bought new shoes and a briefcase, and as he felt he fitted in, his confidence grew. He still did not go out drinking or socialising with colleagues, it was not what he wanted to do. Instead, he focused on his work and continued to study at night and educate himself.

He told me he initially found the language and different regional accents quite challenging. A patient would talk to him about having 'the shits' or 'collywobbles' and he would look up these terms in medical reference books, failing to find them, only to be informed by laughing colleagues that these words were slang or colloquialisms.

He learnt how to understand and cope with all these things. Salt and sugar, where to buy clothes, and understanding patients describing their symptoms. He had close staff members he trusted that he could turn to, for explanations of things he didn't understand. He said he was still learning after all this time.

"Yes, you are," I said. "We are all learning new things all the time, and you will also have learnt from this experience with the nurse."

"What that nurse did to you was wrong. She should not have come to your office. She should not have taken her clothes off. She should not have presented herself naked as she did. Your mind was not programmed to cope with this event, it was out of your scope of experience. Your body was certainly not programmed to cope with it, either. What could you have done? Could you have told her to get dressed and leave?"

"Yes."

"Could you have opened the door?"

"Yes."

"Could you have phoned for security?"

"Yes."

"Could you have shouted out for assistance, a witness?"

"Yes," he said. "I could have done any of these things, but I did not. Instead, I dishonoured myself and my wife."

I explained to him that sometimes it's easier to think of actions you could have taken, or things you could have said or done, after the event, when you're not caught up in the situation. Particularly if this is the first time that you have been placed in such a situation.

I explained that his 'willy' did not have a brain to think with. It did not have morals or a conscience. It just did what it did.

I explained that because his body had never been in a situation like that before, he didn't know how to react. How was your body supposed to react? Just as you had to find out the right way to do things when you first arrived, and in the same way you made alterations with your clothes, hair, food, and language, you also have the responsibility of caring for the well-being of your body so it can follow your wishes, beliefs, culture, and lifestyle.

I asked him if he thought that he would ever react like that again.

He looked horrified, "No!"

I asked him what he thought the nurse had been trying to achieve that night.

He told me he didn't know why she had approached him like that. He'd only ever had a respectful professional relationship with her, and she was not someone with whom he had a lot of contact. He'd also feared that she could have given him a sexually transmitted disease, which he did not wish to pass on to his wife.

I ran some thoughts by him.

I said maybe the nurse admired him because he was such a good man, and she knew he was a good husband and father. Perhaps she wanted some of those qualities in a man in her life. I said we would never know the real reasons which had prompted her to behave like that. I told the doctor I felt that the nurse was much more in need of therapy than he was. That nurse would have to live with the knowledge that she had behaved badly and done the wrong thing, for the rest of her life.

I told the doctor he was a good man, a loving husband, a good father, and a respected medical practitioner. I told him that although the event had been disturbing and confronting, it had not ruined him, and this one event should not define him. I told him that this event had instead given him one more experience to understand and to learn from.

He asked if he should tell his wife what had happened and what he had done.

I pointed out that he had not done what he did, deliberately. He had not wished for it, had not sought the nurse out, or encouraged her in any way. He had not made the event happen; he had been the victim of someone else's calculated actions.

I said that I believed that telling his wife about the incident would only shock and hurt her further, and she was blameless in all of this and did not deserve any more hurt. He agreed he needed to forgive himself and move forward.

He told me had been to a clinic in the city to be tested anonymously. He was relieved to be told that he did not have any sexual diseases. He had spoken to a colleague regarding a 'client of mine' who had penetrated a woman but had not 'planted his seed,' regarding pregnancy, and he had been reassured that there would be no pregnancy.

He decided not to burden his wife with the knowledge of the event. He would instead use this experience to be a better husband and father and would help teach his children how to be better prepared on their journey to adult life.

He'd had his free consultation. He left after thanking me and shaking my hand again. I locked up and went home exhausted.

The next morning my secretary told me there was a strange message from the foreign doctor on the answering phone. She couldn't understand quite what he was saying. Could I please come down and listen to the message?

I replayed the tape.

"Thank you, Madam," the voice said. "I want to let you know that my willy is working very well!"

I was happy for them both.

Footnote

I did not hypnotise the doctor. I had no need to. He was already in a high state of suggestibility following the glowing report he had been given about my therapy from his colleague.

By talking to him and helping him realise that he had been a victim of the nurse, he was able to forgive himself for his uncharacteristic action.

The doctor could now allow this event to become a learning experience, rather than become a life changing problem, which not only made him sexually dysfunctional, but which could have destroyed him, his career, his marriage, and family.

17

THE POWER OF LOVE

My next client walked in smiling, she looked happy, and she was! It was a pleasant change from some of the clients who came to see me. She told me excitedly that she was getting married soon, to her perfect man. They hadn't known each other for long but they both knew immediately when they met, that they had found their soulmate.

Wedding arrangements had been made, the dress had been bought, bridesmaids organised, and the hotel booked. Invitations had been sent and flowers chosen. It was all arranged, even the honeymoon was paid for. The only thing she was not happy about was her size. She had bought her wedding dress two sizes smaller than she actually was, determined to get into it by the wedding day. Unfortunately, despite her best efforts and every good intention, she was finding it impossible to lose weight.

My client had tried diet shakes but hated the taste. She had joined a slimming club but could not always attend the meetings because of work. She was a nurse in a nursing home, and there were always sweets and biscuits around and she had no willpower.

When she got home exhausted from work, she just wanted something quick to eat and often got a takeaway on her way home. Her fiancé wasn't bothered about her weight, he loved her the way she was, but she wanted to look the way that she had done a few years previously. She was on her feet all day, every day, and was exhausted by the time she got home, so didn't do any activities or sports or exercise that could have helped her to lose weight.

What she wanted was to be hypnotised to stop eating the wrong foods and snacking, and to start to exercise on her days off. That's what she wanted, so, that's what she got!

She was a very good subject and went into a deep trance. I was able to give her a lot of positive suggestions.

The foods that you want, the foods that you enjoy, will be those foods that are good for you. Allowing your body to feel satisfied.

Now that your body feels satisfied with these tasty, healthy foods, finding that you have more energy.

And you will enjoy and use this new energy by finding those activities that burn calories, allowing your body to become slimmer, fitter, more attractive.

And just imagine that special wedding day, your day, your groom, that hotel, those bridesmaids, the beautiful flowers, and yes, the dress. The dress.

See yourself in your dress, in front of a long mirror. See yourself from the front, and over your shoulder, from the back. Let your hands run over your shape, the shape you want to be, that you will be.

Her hands ran over her body, as she sat in the chair, smoothing down her imaginary wedding dress, and she smiled, visualising how it would be.

I continued… *See those family members and friends admiring you. So happy for you on your wedding day, and all the difference this difference makes to your day, your wedding, your life, as your body knows how to care enough about you, to care enough about yourself.*

And when your mind and your body is ready to accept all these things, then and only then, your eyes will open, into the here and now.

When she finally came out of trance and opened her eyes, she looked even happier. She was so positive, and felt sure that she would be able to succeed this time. We made an appointment for the same time the following week.

The following week, she had already lost weight. She told me it had been amazing, she hadn't been able to even look at the cakes, biscuits, and sweets at work. She was enjoying salads and fruit and meals that were easy to make when she got home and hadn't had a takeaway meal all week. She had lost four pounds of weight already and was sure she would be the weight she wanted to be, in time for her wedding day.

I felt she was on the right track, so I gave her a CD containing similar kinds of positive suggestions about food, exercise and respecting her body, that I had talked about during our hypnotherapy session. I told her she must never play it while driving or using machinery. She should not lend it to anyone else as it might not be the right suggestions for them. I told her to play it while relaxing at home, making a special time just before going to sleep would be best. If she fell asleep during the CD, then that would not be a problem, she would still hear it and she would just wake up when she chose to wake up.

She thanked me again, promised to keep in touch, and said she would send me a wedding photo of her in the dress. I didn't hear from her, and I never got that photo… but I did hear about her.

A few months later, I got a phone call from a doctor at a rehab hospital about two hours away. My client was a patient there, having been involved in a terrible accident some months earlier. She was now paralysed from the neck down. Her injuries had been treated, but she was extremely depressed, and they were unable to treat the depression effectively.

I was shocked to hear what had happened to her. The doctor told me that she was regularly visited by her fiancé, family and friends, but that she could see no future for herself. I was informed that the only relief she got was by having someone play her weight loss CD to her. Her fiancé had brought it in. She listened to it every day, sometimes several times a day. It was as though it took her to another place. The doctor asked if I would be able to come and visit her, and of course, I agreed.

It was arranged for me to go the next weekend. I found myself at the hospital overlooking the sea. It was a wonderful location. I went inside and was met by friendly staff. It was like no other hospital I had ever visited.

I was upset to see my happy, positive, vibrant lady in a hospital ward, immobile and with such sad eyes. I sat with her and held her hand. She hadn't been told I was coming and was surprised to see me. She talked and cried. She told me she'd been happy with her weight loss, and had started going to line dancing which she loved.

As the wedding day approached, she was feeling so well that she had taken on extra work. She worked in a nursing home during the day, then went on her motorbike to another nursing home to do an overnight shift. She was making good money and looking forward to the wedding and the honeymoon.

Then one night on the way to her second job, her motorbike hit ice on the road. It skidded and went into a deep ditch, and she was trapped underneath, unable to move. She was in agony. It was freezing cold. Night came, then the next day, then it was night again. She missed her shifts, but each place thought she was working at the other job. Her fiancé was frantic when he couldn't contact her. She shouted and shouted for help, but nobody came. She heard vehicles passing by but no one stopped. She was sure she was going to die.

The search was underway, and she was eventually found unconscious in the ditch by her fiancé, who in desperation, on foot ,followed the route he knew she would have taken. She was transported to the local hospital, then soon after had been flown to the specialist hospital. She didn't remember much about this time, she had been heavily sedated.

Her spine had been severed. She would never move again. She had gone from being a nurse who cared for others, to someone who now needed nursing for the rest of her life. She could do nothing for herself, and never would. She felt her life was over. She would never wear THE dress.

She told me, through tears, that her fiancé still wanted to marry her, but she saw no future for them. She was worried he just felt pity for her, and didn't want to trap him in what she perceived as a hopeless situation. She loved him enough to give him back his freedom.

The doctor who had phoned me came in. He was lovely, so caring. He held her other hand and sat with us. He was interested to know how my CD about weight loss could give her such peace when they could not get the same results with their treatment or medications.

I explained that even though the suggestions on the CD were now totally inappropriate for my clients situation as she lay paralysed in bed; *"exercise more, prepare healthy food"* etc, the CD worked, bringing her much-needed relief at an unconscious level.

She asked me if I could hypnotise her again. I looked to the doctor for advice, and he nodded and said that it would be fine.

As I began the induction, she relaxed and slipped into a deep trance.

I lowered my voice and speaking slowly and gently told her…

You have a body, but you are not that body.
Your body is your outer shell.
It protects you from the outer world.
Your body can be fat or thin,
hungry or satisfied.
It can be sick or well,
Whole or broken.

You have a body,
but you are not that body.

You have a mind,
but you are not that mind
You can think, remember, know, and understand.
You have a mind,
but you are not that mind.

You have emotions, but you are not those emotions.
You can be sad or happy,
hopeful or despairing,
frightened or brave.

You have emotions
but you are not those emotions.

So, who are you?

Well,
you are the very centre of will

*and you are capable
of mastering and directing
your body,
your mind
and your emotions,
to be what you want to be,
to know what you need to know,
and to feel what you need to feel.*

*You are a constant and unchanging self.
And you can care enough about yourself
to care enough about yourself
in a way that is just right for you,
and for every part of you
and for every part of every part of you.
And all the difference that difference makes
to your life
and your happiness,
and to those who love you.*

*And when you are ready
then and only then,
coming back
safe to the here and now
in this room
and knowing all about
what needs to happen next.*

I could see Rapid Eye Movement behind her closed eyelids.
It went on and on.
It seemed like a very long time, much longer than would be usual.
The doctor looked at me and raised his eyebrows, I continued waiting in the silence.
I heard gentle shuffling from behind me and turning around I found to my amazement we had been joined by six medical staff who stood at the end of the bed and in the doorway. Some were crying.

After about five minutes of nothing happening, her breathing finally changed, and she opened her eyes and smiled. The doctor looked relieved, he was still holding her hand.

She said, "I must have got you worried there for a bit! I was deciding if I wanted to come back or not. I felt myself floating outside my body. I looked down at myself and said, 'What are you doing, you need to marry the man you love, and you have a dress to get into.' So, I took pity on my body and decided to live. I could have let go, but I didn't want to. I thought I wanted to die, but I don't."

The staff started to drift away, there were red eyes, sniffing and a palpable feeling of relief and hope.

I stayed a bit longer, holding her hand. Her fiancé was coming to visit her shortly. I told her she could get someone to contact me if she needed me to come back again or wanted to talk.

Over the next few months, I occasionally sent her cards and messages. Then one day I received a message from my secretary. My client had phoned, and I had been cordially invited to afternoon tea!

I arrived at the given address with flowers. It was a specially designed disability unit, and I was met at the door by her carer, a lovely lady who was now her friend. She told me they went out during the day to the movies, shopping or visiting friends. My client had an amazing, motorised wheelchair that allowed her to get about, and after being stuck in bed for so long she relished the independence. She was looked after during the day by this carer, as her husband was out at work. She had married her fiancé, and they were very happy together. When he got home from work, he took over from the carer, cooking and looking after her and they were as much in love as ever.

She told me she still had good days and bad days. In hospital, she had found that after using my CD, she was able to imagine my voice and words, and could silently put herself into a trance and give herself any positive suggestions she needed, there and then, to help her through every dark time.

As I followed her through to the lounge, there on the wall in pride of place was the most beautiful canvas photograph of her wedding day. It was a full-length portrait of my lovely client, smiling in the arms of her husband, she was wearing the wedding dress that she had so badly wanted to wear.

Dreams can come true, and love can conquer all.

Footnote

There was a point when my client was hypnotised in hospital when I felt that she might have decided not to come back. None of us would know until faced with such circumstances, what our own choice would be.

I was aware of the risk I was taking when I hypnotised her, but I felt I knew her well enough to believe she would choose the future with her soulmate that she had planned and told me about, rather than the alternative.

I wondered if I would have worked differently and chosen different words, had I known that behind me was an audience of professional medical people. They were there out of concern for my client, interest in the process of hypnosis, which they could see gave her a relief that their treatments and medications could not provide. Ultimately, I believe, they were there because they cared. My client was such a wonderful person, that I think we all wanted the same positive outcome for her, however that came about.

18

MORE THAN WORDS CAN SAY

My secretary had left work early because a huge winter storm was looming. It was only mid-afternoon, but the sky was already black, it was extremely windy, and it looked as though we were in for a lot of rain.

The lady I was expecting next for her first appointment with me had left her phone number, but my secretary had been unable to contact her before she left, to cancel the appointment. I knew nothing about this new client except my secretary had said she was middle-aged, had come in person to make the appointment and that it had been difficult to understand her because she whispered!

The appointment time came and went, the heavens opened, and rain was lashing at the windows. I put an extra log on the fire in the waiting room downstairs and decided to stay a bit longer and catch up on some paperwork. I hoped the storm would move on so I wouldn't get soaked walking to my car.

I was settled in a comfortable chair by the fire with a mug of tea when I was startled by a loud banging on the door. I opened the door and to my astonishment there stood a policeman in a waterproof cape. He was drenched and holding onto the arm of a weeping lady clutching an inside-out umbrella who was also soaked through.

I quickly ushered them both in and closed the door on the weather. They stood dripping onto my stone floor as the policeman explained he had found this lady lost and very distressed. She hadn't been able to talk very much but she handed him the appointment card with my address on it, so he decided to bring her to me.

I got them to hang up their rain-soaked outer clothes, gave them a towel each and made them both a mug of tea. He was such a kind young man and said he thought the lady had got off her bus at the wrong stop and became disorientated in the rain. She listened and nodded.

I took her upstairs and then came back down and told the policeman he was welcome to dry off by the fire and finish his tea but I asked him to make sure the front door was locked if he left before we came back down. He thanked me and sat down with his mug; feet stretched out towards the fire, I noticed he was trying to fix the umbrella.

I went back upstairs. By now my client had calmed down a bit, so I asked her how I could help.

She took a notebook and pen out of her bag and wrote,

I have lost my voice.

I continued asking her questions and she continued writing me answers. Sometimes she attempted to reply in a raspy whisper which seemed to be painful and a big effort for her. She nodded and shook her head, and we did our best to communicate.

I learnt she had been an English teacher but was forced to leave the job she loved when she lost her voice. Her husband was much older, retired, and hard of hearing, which was why she now used the pen and paper, it was the quickest way for her to be understood.

I asked how long she had been like this.

About 3 years!

She wrote that she had seen her doctor about the condition, and he had sent her to specialists. She was still seeing a speech therapist, but in all this time there had been no improvement with her voice.

She became very emotional and wrote.

Within the space of 3 years my life has changed so dramatically, that now I hardly recognise myself.

She wrote that her husband hadn't wanted her to come for the appointment because of the weather. He had been unable to drive her because of his failing eyesight which made it impossible for him to drive in the dark, but she had been determined to make the appointment and had caught the bus. Unfortunately, she had mistakenly got off at the wrong stop.

I heard the front door open then close and excused myself and went downstairs to check the policeman had locked the door – he had. The umbrella was fixed and drying opened by the fire. The downstairs waiting room was inviting and warm with the crackling fire and table lamps. I drew the curtains, went back upstairs, and suggested that we move downstairs to be more comfortable. I was aware the remaining appointments for that day had been cancelled and knew we would not be disturbed, the answering machine would pick up any incoming messages.

My client came downstairs, took off her wet shoes and sat by the fire holding her mug of tea. It was then that I asked her what had been happening about three years ago when she first started having problems with her voice.

She looked at me and started crying.

In a strained whisper, she told me she was married with twin girls who were grown up now. One had a good job that she loved and for a time had continued to live at home with them. The other daughter had gone away to Scotland to study medicine. It had been a difficult time for the girls when they were first separated, as they had always been together, but now they each had to follow their own paths.

Then the daughter, who was in Scotland, told them she had a serious boyfriend and asked if he could come home with her for Christmas. He had, and he was wonderful, the family loved him, and they all got on well together. After the holiday the couple returned to Scotland and the other daughter had been invited to visit them over the Easter Holiday. So, a few months later she went by train. She was met at the station by her sister and her partner, and with them was his identical twin brother!

It ended up, a year later, with the twin sisters engaged to the twin brothers. At this point, my client said she felt as though a rug had been pulled out from underneath her. Both her girls were now away with their new partners, and her home felt empty.

The girls came to visit, and they asked if she could help them arrange a double wedding in their local Parish Church where they had always worshipped. She had been totally included in all decisions, was extremely busy and happy with all the wedding preparations and was still teaching at this time.

After the weddings, both girls left with their husbands, and it was at this point that her voice left her.

She was really crying now as she wrote.

> *I thought I was just overtired or coming down with something. As a teacher I was used to projecting my voice in the classroom and had occasionally strained it, but I have never experienced anything like this. I expected my voice would return, but it didn't.*

I asked, "What was it like for you, once both girls left home?"

She looked at me with tears rolling down her cheeks and said, in a normal voice.

"I miss them, more than words can say."

I was not even sure that she was aware that she had just spoken, or that she had explained the reason for her loss of voice.

She continued talking.

"The home we live in now is old and much too large for the two of us. It belonged to my parents, and we inherited it. It's full of antique furniture and beautifully decorated in keeping with the house, but it's not to my taste. The garden is established but very large, and it's becoming too much for my husband to manage now."

"What would you like to have happen?" I asked.

"I would like to sell the house," she said. "I want to move up to Scotland to be near my daughters. There's a baby on the way and I want to be there for them. Both my daughters have suggested it already."

"And what does your husband think of the idea?" I asked.

"He doesn't think that I would ever leave the family home, my friends, and life here, but I'm not bothered about leaving any of those things, I just want to be closer to my girls."

"And have you told him how you feel?" I asked.

"No," she replied. "He always makes the decisions; I have no say in them."

I asked if she thought he was saying that she wanted to stay in the house because he didn't want to leave it? Did she think that he would be willing to sell?

She nodded and told me that her husband was retired, his best friend had recently died, and he no longer kept up with old business contacts or played golf anymore, because of his poor health and failing eyesight. There were no family ties for him to the area. She thought that it would be better for him not to have the worry of the upkeep of the big house and gardens.

"I think he really misses the girls too." She said.

"Are you aware that you have been talking to me normally for the last few minutes?" I smiled.

Her eyes opened wide, and her hands went over her mouth.

"Goodness! Yes I have, haven't I!" She exclaimed.

I said that now she had found her voice, her voice could and should be heard. I told her that I was pleased she had been able to speak to me, but I believed that she needed to be having this conversation about what she wanted to happen next, with her husband. It was important she had an equal say in what happened for their future. There was a lot to be discussed but it would be much easier to do that now that she had found her voice.

I suggested that perhaps they could go and visit their daughters and see how they felt about being in Scotland before they made any major decisions about moving there permanently.

I said, "If you always do what you have always done, you will always get what you've always got – so do something different!"

She smiled and nodded.

The rain was easing off now.

I told her I would like to drive her home, she was only just drying out. I suggested she ring her husband – who must be worried about her being out for so long in this awful weather. She said that would be a good idea.

I switched off the answering machine and she used the office phone to ring home; it was picked up immediately.

"It's me!" she said, loud and clear.

Silence.

"Can you hear me?"

Silence.

"I wanted to let you know the therapist is driving me home because it's still raining, I'll see you soon."

Silence.

Then he spoke her name.

"Yes," she said, "I'm here, it's me. We'll talk when I get home. Love you, bye!"

The rain turned to drizzle as I switched the answering machine back on, locked up and set off for the car park. My client was still talking, catching up for lost time. As we sat in the car she said her husband wouldn't know what had hit him when she got home! She said her voice had been silent for the last three years, but she felt that she had been silenced for much longer than that.

I asked her to explain.

"My husband taught both our girls how to drive. I told him that I would like to learn too, but he said that I didn't need to learn because he would always be able to take me everywhere. He even used to drop me off at school and pick me up again and we always do all the shopping together."

Tonight, had proved to her that he couldn't always take her when and where she wanted to go. She asked me if I thought she was too old to be able to learn to drive.

I laughed and told her about my mother.

My mother had been over sixty when, for the first time in her life, she inherited money. At that time, she didn't even have a bank account or access to an account. She was given housekeeping money by my father each week and she had to manage it.

When she received the inheritance cheque she declared that she was going to open a bank account. Then she said she was going to learn to drive and she was going to buy herself a car.

"Don't be silly," said my father. "You are a woman You don't need a car!"

Nonetheless, that's exactly what my mother did. She paid for lessons and passed her driving test first time. A friend's husband helped her buy a Morris Minor. It was then that she decided it would be easier to get in and out of the car if she wasn't wearing a skirt. What she needed, she thought, were some comfortable and practical 'slacks' (trousers).

She bought the slacks and when my father first saw her wearing them, he was outraged and said, "You can't wear those – I used to be the mayor!"

My mother ignored him and bought more pairs of drip dry, non-iron, brown and beige slacks with elasticated waists – she felt liberated!

Some years later, my father retired and with retirement, he lost the use of the company car. At this point he was reduced to asking my mother if he could borrow her car when he needed transport. Graciously she allowed him to, but she always made him, "top up the tank."

My client was still laughing as she got out of the car and thanked me. Her husband was waiting for her at the open front door.

I really would have liked to have known what happened. I hope her husband shared her excitement for the journey ahead into their future. All I'd been asked to do that evening was to help her find her voice, and thankfully I'd been able to do just that!

Footnote

I was beginning to feel vulnerable when working late on my own with clients in the evening. Working late was something I had always done, as many of my clients were only free to see me after they finished work, but I'd had a few clients recently who made me feel uncomfortable or who had behaved quite aggressively in the sessions. I felt I should be taking more notice of my personal safety.

It all came to a head one night when I was working late in my private practice, which was in a little old two storey stone cottage, tucked away down a cobbled yard that cut through to the main bus station. There were no neighbours either side, which was great for client privacy, but not so good for my personal safety.

This late-night appointment was with an existing male client who came to stop smoking. My secretary had left for the night, and I was upstairs with my hypnotised client who was lying relaxed deep in trance in the reclined leather chair.

I heard the front door open and close, and the sound of two sets of footsteps below. I was not expecting anyone. If prospective clients wanted information, there were leaflets in a rack outside the front door describing some of the more common conditions that hypnotherapy could treat effectively. In general, people only came in if they wanted to make an appointment or if they were attending an already scheduled appointment. I knew I had no one else booked in for that evening.

I heard two deep male voices talking softly, and I mentally kicked myself for being careless in leaving the front door unlocked that evening, even though I'd been doing just that for years, with no incident.

I heard the scrape of drawers opening and closing. I sat frozen, silent, listening. My client remained reclined and completely oblivious to what was happening downstairs.

The footsteps moved into the kitchen area which was directly below me. Again, I could hear drawers and cupboard doors opening and closing. They were definitely looking for something – I knew that my premises was in the process of being burgled.

I heard footsteps on the creaky staircase, they were both coming upstairs.

My client was still reclining peacefully, deep in trance.

So, I told him in a calm voice that I was leaving the room and he could stay relaxed for as long as he wanted to, but he could also wake up if he felt he needed to. This was a safety measure so if, for example, I screamed, or someone threatened him, he would have left trance immediately and been able to respond appropriately.

I stood and quietly opened the door and looked down to find two huge men creeping up the stairs. I smiled politely at them, turned back into the room, and said loudly, "Would you both please excuse me for a moment – I'll be back as soon as I can."

Then I shut the door behind me and stood on the landing looking at the two men. I could smell alcohol coming off them.

To say they were surprised to find me there would be an understatement. I think, with the subdued lighting downstairs, they must have thought the property was unoccupied. They obviously had not expected to find anyone there working so late.

"Can I help you?" I asked.

They looked at each other, then one said, "We've come to find out about the hydrotherapy."

"Excellent." I said, "You have come to the right place! I have some leaflets downstairs which might be helpful, shall we go down and I'll get you some?"

They nodded then turned and clattered noisily back down the stairs.

"I'll be with you both in a minute!" I shouted over my shoulder to my still oblivious client as I followed them.

I took some leaflets from my secretary's desk and passed them over, "I can't be long," I said to the men. "My clients need to get back to the gym, but these leaflets will give you some information."

"It's probably best if you ring the number on the front tomorrow, and my secretary can arrange for you both to come in for a consultation, where we can discuss things in more detail. There is no charge for the first consultation, it's free."

They took the proffered leaflets, never looking me in the eye, mumbled their thanks, turned, opened the door, and left the cottage, walking unsteadily down the cobbled yard. I engaged the lock behind them and drew the curtains.

My heart was pounding, and I started shaking. I looked around. Drawers were open, cushions were overturned, kitchen cupboards were ajar, the desk had been moved. I couldn't see if anything was missing, I was just grateful the men had left the premises without the situation escalating.

I took some deep breaths and then shut the drawers, replaced the cushions, and went back upstairs to my abandoned client who was still reclining comfortably, deep in trance, exactly as I had left him.

We finished the session successfully, and my client left a few minutes later than normal, still blissfully unaware of what had occurred!

I never saw or heard from the two men again, not surprisingly they did not return for their free "hydrotherapy" consultation.

So, when this lady and the policeman arrived in the storm I was happy for the policeman to sit and get warm in front of my fire, it was good to have a police presence at my work. However, when I heard him leave, I had to get up and check the door was locked.

Moving my client from the therapy room upstairs to the much more comfortable and welcoming room downstairs with its subdued lighting and the glow, warmth and crackling of the fire was trance-inducing, like being in a daydream. I believe this relaxed atmosphere with the mesmerising fire, the rain on the windows, and the comforting mug of tea contributed to my client allowing herself to talk openly and freely about her family, her hopes and dreams. There was no need for me to induce trance, she was already in a heightened state of suggestibility.

I'd been amazed when she started talking to me in her normal voice – that she had told me she hadn't been able to use for the last three years. It had seemed so natural for her to do this at this time, that she hadn't even noticed she was doing it, speaking out loud, until I had pointed it out to her!

I felt sure that now she had quite literally found her voice she would have her say, and she and her husband would have that talk. I didn't think that he would be speaking for her any more.

The disturbing incident with the two prowling intruders was one of the deciding factors that would eventually result in my decision to downscale my private practice and work within the National Health System. Working in the NHS consulting rooms, I knew I would never find myself alone and vulnerable without the backup and support of colleagues.

A journey of a thousand miles
begins with a single step.

Ancient Chinese Philosopher Lao Tzu

19

SCARED TO DEATH

I received an urgent phone call in the middle of another busy day. It was from my lovely friend Diane, a colleague from the Drug and Alcohol Department.

She was ringing from the psychiatric unit at the General Hospital, where she'd been called in because a young woman we had both previously worked with had been taken into the hospital by the police the previous night. Our client was reportedly violent, hysterical and had been found in her soaking wet pyjamas, standing under a railway bridge in the pouring rain, at midnight. She had been restrained and sedated. This sounded serious.

Diane said the client had been screaming for me and refused to speak to anyone else. I had to cancel clients and get permission from my manager to attend.

I remembered this lady well. As I drove through to the hospital, I recalled that she was young, happily married with a toddler and a new baby. She was petite and delicate. Unusually, I went to her house to see her in her bed for appointments, as she was too frail to travel into the department for therapy.

Her husband would open the front door and show me up to their bedroom. The bedroom was pink, frilly and flowery with a lot of soft toys and dolls. My client would be sitting up in bed with her childhood teddy, Sally, on the pillow beside her.

The family had a lot of community help for her and the new baby, a beautiful little girl who had been born prematurely. Her husband, who was a kind man, was her carer, and he ran the home, cooking, cleaning, and looking after her and the children with love and devotion.

I couldn't imagine this tiny lady being able to go downstairs unassisted, never mind having the energy to run in her pyjamas in the rain to a railway bridge at night.

As I walked down the hospital corridor, I could hear screaming. I was escorted through a locked door into a secure area. My client was in a hospital robe lying on a bed, being restrained by five nurses. One for each limb and one man lying over her body, holding her down as she thrashed and screamed. I was shocked, it was like a scene from a horror movie.

Diane was there, she looked relieved to see me. I saw a chair and I put it beside the bed. I gently held my client's right hand and got the nurse to release her arm. I spoke softly to her, and her eyes moved towards me. I have never seen such terror in anyone's eyes before. Her body was arched and in spasm, and she was still trying to kick out and free herself from being held down by the nurses. I don't know where she found the strength, it just didn't seem possible.

I continued talking softly.

"This must be very frightening for you... I'd really like to help if you would let me."

Her eyes were pleading.

Her legs were still trying to kick, but her other arm was more relaxed.

"Would you like your left arm to be free?"

She nodded.

I looked at the nurse who reluctantly relinquished her hold on the left arm and stood back a little.

"Is that better?"

She nodded again.

I began to slow my breathing down and she gradually matched her breathing to mine. She calmed down and stopped trying to kick.

"Would you like your legs to be released?"

She nodded.

They let go and stood back and she lay still on the bed, she didn't kick.

"That's better," I said.

I let out a sigh, and she sighed.

"Would you like the weight off your body?"

She nodded again.

The male nurse slowly released her.

She lay there holding my hand, she was calm but had tears in her eyes.

Then she spoke to me, whispering in a low voice, "They are doing the Devil's work."

I asked the nurses to wait outside.

The nurses looked at each other, they were not sure what to do. I don't think they wanted to leave me alone with her. It had taken five of them to restrain her before, but Diane encouraged them to move to the doorway, where they stood silently, observing.

I spoke gently, as I had done in previous hypnotherapy sessions, and she responded by closing her eyes and entering trance.

And when they are doing the Devil's work, how are they doing the Devil's work? I asked

"They won't let me run!"

And when you can run, where can you run to?

"I run to safety."

And when you run to safety... where do you run to?

"I run to the bridge... so the Devil can't catch me... and hurt my family."

Her body tensed again, she was still deep in trance, but her eyes opened, she gripped my hand tightly and she looked terrified.

What's happening now? I asked.

"The Devil... is here," she whispered.

I kept holding her hand and whispered back

... And when the Devil is here... where IS the Devil when the Devil is here?

"On my legs," she whispered

And then what happens?

"It's purple... and I can't move," she closed her eyes.

And when it's purple and you can't move... it's purple like what?

I was looking for a metaphor, something that would help me understand what the purple could be, but my client just repeated "purple."

She whispered again, "Purple is crawling up my legs."
I continued with purple.
And as purple crawls higher up your legs, what happens next?
"Purple gets my fanny."
And as purple gets your fanny, then what happens?
"It's on top of my body and I can't breathe."
And when it's on top of your body and you can't breathe… then what happens?
"I can't swallow."
And when you can't breathe, and when you can't swallow… what happens next?
She whispered, "I die."
I acknowledged her dreadful statement.
And… you… die.
There was movement in the doorway, the staff pressed forward. I was aware of Diane cautioning them back so they didn't interfere with what was happening, it went quiet.
I still held my client's hand, but she was no longer gripping mine.
I couldn't see her chest moving.
I couldn't hear her breathing.
I waited in the silence… Finally, I spoke.
… And… how long do you die for?
She gasped in air and said, "I can breathe now."
And what is the first thing you notice when you can breathe now?
"There is no weight on my chest."
And… there is no weight on your chest.
"Purple is sliding down my body. It is lighter. It's lavender."
And when purple slides down your body and becomes lavender now… what does lavender do?
"It is turning white and silky … and it slips off me onto the floor."
And as white and silky slips off you onto the floor… what difference does that make?
"I can breathe."
Her eyes opened, she had spontaneously left trance, and I helped her to sit up on the edge of the bed, she was so petite that her feet did not touch the floor.

I helped her off the bed. The hospital staff were still standing in the doorway. They looked as though they were not sure about what they'd just witnessed, but they also looked relieved she was upright, calm, and talking normally.

"I need a cup of tea," she said.

We moved through to a sitting area. Someone went to get us both a cup of tea. She said she was exhausted and needed to sleep. I said I thought sleep was an excellent idea.

We sat and drank the tea. She thanked me for coming to save her. I said I'd been glad to come and was pleased I'd been able to help. I told her I had been distressed to see her in such a state.

"I need to sleep now." She said. "But can you come back tomorrow please; I have some things that I want to tell you."

I agreed but said that it would have to be after work. The staff said that it would be fine.

As I left, I felt that I got some funny looks!

The next afternoon I arrived to find my client sitting in the main ward, dressed with her hair done and face made up. She was clutching a teddy which I recognised as Sally, her bear from home, which had been brought in by her husband. Diane had already been in to see her too. We were brought more cups of tea, then she started to talk.

I sat and listened.

"I was an only child in a very unhappy home. My father worked in the shipyard, and he was always tired and angry. He talked about God all the time and we lived by the Ten Commandments. Every day it was God, Sin, Satan, Hell and Damnation. We prayed every day and as a family we spent hours in Church every Sunday. My role was to be a good girl and not bring shame to my family. My mother was a small quiet woman who never had a say about anything, we both had to obey my father. It was miserable."

She had been sent to a Catholic School where the nuns were unkind and frightening. She left school as soon as she could and got a job working with a friend in a shop. She enjoyed it and earned money for the first time in her life but had to take home the unopened wage packet each week to her father. He then gave her pocket money back.

"It wasn't fair," she said, "I earned it and wanted to spend it like my friends did, on going out to the pictures or buying new clothes."

She had remained a good girl until one evening on the way home from work, she met a sailor. He was funny, kind, handsome and wore a smart uniform. His ship was in the docks getting repaired. He walked with her most of the way home, but she wouldn't let him come to the door.

"I didn't want my dad to see him," she said, "I knew he wouldn't approve and he'd be angry."

They arranged to meet again each evening after work, and he would walk with her nearly all the way home. He talked to her and made her laugh and feel special for the first time in her life.

At the weekend she lied and told her father she wanted to go and see a film with her friend. She told him she had been invited to sleep over afterwards by her friend's mother, so she wouldn't have to walk home alone in the dark. Her father surprisingly, agreed to let her go.

That night she didn't meet up with her friend, and she didn't go to a film. Instead, she met up with her sailor, and she stopped being a good girl. And not being a good girl was wonderful, she was completely in love.

Her sailor told her his ship was leaving the following week and asked if he could have her address so he could keep in touch and write to her. She knew this would not be possible, she was terrified her father would open the letters and find out she had been meeting up with a man.

They had to say goodbye. Her heart was broken. She had felt truly loved for the first time in her life.

Then the morning sickness started.

Her mother noticed and took her to the doctor.

The doctor confirmed that she was pregnant.

Her mother was horrified, and she was terrified.

What would her father say?

Her father said nothing, he beat her.

When he did speak, he called her terrible names and told her she would burn in Hell. He told her she was ruined and no one would ever want her. He said she had brought dreadful shame upon the family and he wouldn't be able to hold his head up in church. Then he called in the Priest.

The Priest declared her a wicked, sinful, fallen woman and confirmed that she would indeed burn in Hell. "There is nowhere for you to run and hide, God sees all, and the Devil is coming for you!"

The Priest and her father decided she should be sent immediately to a Catholic Home for naughty girls, before the pregnancy began to show, so that no one would find out.

She was informed, that after the birth, the baby would be taken away and adopted, and then she would be allowed to come back home, and the whole unpleasant sinful situation would never be spoken of again. She was given no choice in the matter, and she felt totally alone.

Her parents never asked who the father was, however, the Priest did ask if he was a Catholic. She told them nothing. Her mother said nothing. Then, because her face was bruised and damaged from her father's beating, and she was suffering morning sickness and unable to go into work, she lost her job.

Desperate, she did the only thing that she could think of, she waited until her father was at work and her mother had gone out shopping, then searched the entire house for money. She found the rent money, the coal money, the insurance money, the housekeeping money, and took it all. She believed that she was owed it from all the wages that had been taken from her. She packed her few possessions in a bag, with a packet of biscuits and her teddy bear Sally and left the house for good. She ran.

That night she ended up in an unknown part of town. It began pouring with rain, so she waited under a railway bridge, where other homeless people were sheltering. She was frightened, but some women were kind to her. One lent her a blanket, another shared some food, and she sat with them by a fire under the bridge. They noticed her bruised face and she told them some of her story. They advised that because she was so young and pregnant, she would be able to get help. They explained what to do and where to go and advised her not to give anyone her real name or address because if she did, there was a risk that she would be returned home as a runaway.

After a sleepless night, she had gone to Social Services to ask for assistance. She did not give them her name or address. Her face was still swollen and bruised from the beating her father had given her. The social workers could see that she had come from a bad situation and when they discovered that she was also pregnant, she was immediately given help and placed into a hostel.

The social workers helped her to relocate to another town to start again. She was put on a train and given money; she had never been on a train before and had never left her town. Strangers from Social Services looked after her better than her own parents ever had, meeting her at the destination and taking her to a fully furnished flat. She received medical care and everything that was needed for the baby's arrival. At the age of just sixteen she made a complete fresh start. She was alone but never regretted leaving, and never contacted her parents or friends.

Months later she gave birth to a beautiful baby boy and loved him immediately. She was very frail following the birth and she continued to be helped financially and practically by Social Services.

One day when she was pushing her son in his pram in the park, a man spoke to her. He was kind to them both and would eventually become her husband, loving her son as his own. He had no family, and she had no contact with her family, so they got married on their own in a Registry Office. He gave up his job working in the community and became her full-time carer.

"I really regret getting married at the Registry," she told me "I know it's legal, but I don't know how God would view it. I always dreamt that I would have a traditional Church wedding one day, it's just the way I was brought up."

Soon she became pregnant again. Her doctor had warned her against this, as she was still frail and recovering from the first baby, but she never considered contraception or termination, the strong Catholic influence of her early religious learning was still with her.

Their baby daughter was born prematurely. She was small, sickly, and once again Social Services provided amazing support. Through all of these times, she had been prescribed ever-increasing doses of medication, and it was then that Diane and I had first become involved. My role was to help in her withdrawal from benzodiazepines, as it was felt by her doctor that she now needed to reduce her dependency on medications, and this I had done successfully.

In all the sessions that I had seen her, she had never before revealed this part of her life. She explained that she'd wanted to tell me her story for a long time but had felt unable to but was glad to be telling me now. She revealed with some embarrassment that she had a stronger sex drive than her husband. He was always concerned for her health and wellbeing and was aware of the risks of her falling pregnant again. She didn't care about the consequences of their lovemaking, she just wanted to feel loved. After she'd had her way, and her husband was asleep, was when she remembered the priest's words, and knew that she had sinned and the Devil would come to get her. So, without disturbing her sleeping husband, she would slip out of their bed and run through the night to the sanctuary of the railway bridge. Her husband would later wake to realise she had gone, and he would ring the police.

When she ran, her husband would remain at home to look after the children and wait for her to be returned. The police knew exactly where to find her, under the local railway bridge, that was where she always went. The police would then drop her safely home, by which time her terror and the need to run, would have passed.

This last time however, it had unfortunately been different policemen who had responded to her husband's phone call when he reported her missing. These police officers didn't know her or her history of running away, and they followed procedure. Instead of dropping her back home they took her directly to the hospital.

She tried to tell the police she was running from the Devil, but they didn't understand, they thought she was mad. She got more desperate, first reasoning with them, then demanding to be taken home. When they wouldn't listen and take her home, she had become upset and aggressive, which resulted in her being restrained and sedated, and then sent to the psychiatric ward, which is when Diane had been called in.

My client said she and her husband had talked that afternoon and discussed what they wanted to do for their future. She said they had a plan. It was a secret for now, but she would eventually let me know.

However, I never saw her again.

Footnote

It was Diane who eventually let me know what their plan was for the future, she was still working with the family. Years later, after I had retired and moved abroad, Diane let me know that the couple had found a Catholic Priest who agreed to give their marriage a church blessing. I knew this would have been so important to my client who had always wanted to be married in church. Diane had been invited to the blessing and later emailed me a photograph of the family standing on the steps outside the church. Our client wore a long white silky dress that flowed onto the ground, and she held a bouquet of white gypsophila (baby's breath), and lavender-coloured flowers. She looked healthy and extremely happy.

They now had four children, three sons and a daughter, who all celebrated their blessing with them. Sally was there too, held in the arms of their daughter. I remembered the bear and Diane informed me the bear was really called Salvation, Sally for short and our client had named it when she had been just a little girl, as the teddy had always been her Salvation. Diane said that after our session in the ward, the Devil had never returned, and our client had never felt the need to run again.

I was still left with many unanswered questions.

I wondered how her Godfearing father and mother had ever explained to friends, neighbours and people at church the sudden disappearance of their only daughter.

I wondered if my client had ever realised the significance of running to the railway bridge as an adult, when a railway bridge was where she had first found sanctuary at sixteen, when she ran away from home.

I wondered about the significance of purple. I thought about church vestments, I thought about bedding or clothing on someone who had hurt her. I thought about weight on the chest and not being able to breathe or swallow and the purple on the fanny, and the horror of knowing that you couldn't breathe and were going to die.

I wondered about a father who could beat his pregnant daughter and a mother who stood by and did nothing.

I wondered why a little girl would choose to use Salvation as a name for a precious Teddy Bear.

I had my own ideas about all these things, but it was not for me to question or explore.

My beautiful friend Diane who did so much for those she worked with, has since passed away. Diane was one of the kindest, most genuine of people. She really cared and made a huge difference to so many lives. She is greatly missed.

20

DOWN CAME A BLACKBIRD

My next client arrived looking smart, confident, wearing a suit, high heels and carrying a briefcase. She was accompanied by her mother. I was surprised when she asked if her mother could sit in with her during the session. All I knew was that she had come to see me about a phobia.

I said that would be fine.

My client explained she had suffered from this phobia all her life. Her mother was the only person who really knew just how dreadful it was and had always been there for her. As she'd got older, she'd found ways to manage the phobia by avoiding certain situations but could at times still be taken unawares. Her husband knew about the phobia, but he didn't know how serious it was, and had never seen the full effect that it had on her. She had become an expert in avoidance.

I still didn't know what the phobia was, I think giving it a name would have taken her too close to the fear, so I just sat, listened, and let her talk.

"I can't remember a time when I didn't have this phobia. I remember going to a friend's house when I was about six. She had a budgie, and I froze in horror when I saw it. When she let it out of its cage, it flew around the room, and as it flew past me, I started screaming. When it landed on my friends head I had a complete panic attack and had to be taken out of the room."

"I had to go and pick her up!" said her mother.

"You were so traumatised that you couldn't speak for quite some time, you couldn't stop crying, and you never went back to that house again."

My client also recalled a trip to the zoo when she'd been in primary school. It had been a great day, and all was going well, until they were taken to see the birds.

The birds in cages were no problem, the birds walking around the grounds were no problem, the birds out on the ponds were no problem. The problem was the wild birds, who were small enough to fly in and out of the wires of the exotic bird's cages, getting an easy meal. As they fluttered past, she saw the movement, heard the wings, and immediately became hysterical, but this time it was in front of the teachers and all her friends.

She couldn't control herself and couldn't stop crying. A teacher took her away to another part of the zoo to wait for the others to join them. Everyone wanted to know what had happened. She couldn't explain it, but it was really overwhelmingly frightening.

After the zoo experience she avoided going on other school trips. Family holidays were not taken at the seaside, because she was worried about seagulls swooping down on people to steal food. She began to get upset just talking about it to me, and said she felt stupid.

I assured her I didn't think she was stupid, she had obviously been living with this phobia for a very long time.

Her mother interjected. "It's always been like this! I remember once when you were in kindergarten, the class was singing Sing a song of sixpence and when they reached the line 'along came a blackbird and pecked off her nose,' the teacher pretended to peck off your nose with her hand. You had complete hysterics! They had to ring me to come and pick you up because you couldn't stop crying!"

It had been difficult after that to get her to return to kindergarten. Mum explained to the teacher that her daughter had been frightened by the song when she pretended to pull off her nose. Thankfully the teacher was very understanding, and that song was never sung in their class again. My client said she couldn't remember that day, but she was visibly upset just hearing her mother talk about the incident.

"It affects my everyday life in so many ways," my client said, "I work for a bank and at certain times of the year it's a nightmare trying to leave work, because flocks of pigeons gather at dusk, coming into roost, and they're everywhere. Sometimes noisy starlings flock in from the fields, and I can't leave the safety of the bank until they've gone. Luckily, my manager's very understanding."

"The reason that I've come to see you," she said, "is I have just received a promotion which requires me to move to London. It's a good opportunity and my husband is happy to relocate but the branch is close to Trafalgar Square. I have seen photographs of the pigeons being hand fed by tourists there, but because of the proximity to my work I just don't know if I can face all those birds, I don't know if I should accept the position. Do you think you can help?"

I told her that I had been able to help other clients with similar phobias successfully but needed more information first.

"Were there any other times that you can remember being frightened by a bird?" I asked.

Her mother interjected again, "There was an earlier time, but she was very young, she wouldn't remember that one!"

"Can you tell me what happened?" I enquired.

"When she was just a baby, I put her out in the garden to get some fresh air. I left her safely tucked in her pram, with the hood pulled up, under a shady apple tree which was full of blossom. I was also outside, washing the windows, but I was keeping a careful eye out, as the neighbour had a large ginger cat which liked to jump the fence and try and sit in the pram.

"As I was cleaning, I saw movement near the pram and heard her cry out. I rushed across to find a huge black crow inside the hood of the pram flapping and pecking. I screamed and clapped my hands to scare it away. The bird immediately flew off, and I picked her up. She was crying and her head was scratched, but her eyes were safe. We lived near a farm and crows were known to gather when the lambs were being born, and they sometimes plucked out the tiny creatures' eyes. I was so worried that the crow had tried to take my baby's eyes."

My attention had been on the mother as she told this story, but now we both looked at her daughter who was sitting bolt upright. Her eyes were wide open, darting everywhere, but she wasn't seeing us. Her arms were held rigid, straight down, her fingers opening and closing, her mouth moved, then she screamed. Her mother and I jumped in our chairs.

While her mother had been telling the story, my client had listened and automatically slipped into an altered state, regressing back to the time of the incident in the pram. She had no words, no understanding, and no ability to move away from the danger, trapped in the moment, reliving the terror of the incident as she had experienced it as a baby, helpless in her pram.

Luckily, I knew from listening to the mother's story, that my client had survived the trauma of the crow, even if as an adult, she had never consciously remembered the event, so I knew that I could safely move time on.

I lowered my voice and spoke gently to her unconscious mind.

... And you are safe, your mum is here, and the big black bird has gone.

Your mum has got you safe. The big black bird won't come back.

The big black bird was as big as you and the only thing that you could do was cry.

That was the right thing to do because your mum heard you and came running and shouting.

The bird was afraid of your mum, because she was bigger, and it flew away.

And so it is, that you have taken a long time to grow up, and now you are as tall as your mum.

You were only a baby when you were frightened by the big black bird in your pram.

You were only a child when you were frightened by a blackbird in a song.

You were only a child when you were frightened by the budgie at your friend's house.

And you were only a little girl when you were frightened by the birds at the zoo.

*But now, you are **not** a child, you have grown up and you are an adult.*

Birds are not the same size as you.

You are bigger and stronger than birds.

You have learnt so many clever ways to avoid contact with birds and that is wonderful.

No bird has ever touched you since that fateful day.

It may be that you will never like birds, but I know that you no longer need to fear them.

Birds may flap their wings near you, but birds want to avoid you.

You don't have to go to the seaside, but if you did, you could choose not to hold food so that the seagulls would not be interested in you.

You could go to London and watch people feed pigeons in Trafalgar Square, but the birds would not be interested in you, if you had no food.

Perhaps you can take a little time just to think of how many ways you can behave differently around birds, now that you are grown up and you are no longer a child.

And you know now that you are bigger than birds,

and you know now that you don't have to be frightened by birds anymore.

I waited while she sat silently and processed these words.

Eventually, she nodded her head.

I gave more positive reinforcements, then I brought her out of trance, and she sat for a while.

Then she said, "I think I would like to be able to take my niece and nephew to the park to feed the ducks."

"And... do you think you would be able to do that?" I asked.

"I could try." She replied, "I could throw the bread to the ducks, it would be all right if they didn't flap their wings."

"Some ducks might fly in when they see the bread, would that be all right?" I said.

"Yes, as long as they don't touch me, or the children."

"If you felt at any time, they were getting too close, you could simply leave the bread and walk away." I suggested.

Again, she nodded and agreed.

We made an appointment for the following week.

She apologised for her 'funny turn.'

I said it was the best thing that could have happened because now the 'baby' part of her really understood and knew that she was safe.

"It was terrifying for you in the pram as a baby, you were helpless and you have understandably been carrying that terror with you all this time, but now you are an adult you no longer need to fear the fear." I said reassuringly.

My client returned alone the following week.

She smiled and proudly revealed she'd taken her niece and nephew to the park to feed the ducks, on her own without her mother. She'd been apprehensive before going, but once there, she'd felt no fear, and just joined in the fun. There were even some big geese and swans, and she'd been able to feed them too, thankfully they had stayed in the water.

"I've been thinking about my phobia," she said. "It's not just about the birds, it's also to do with light. I have always hated and feared the moment that daylight fades to dark. Even switching off a light triggers this extreme anxiety and panic. Living with this fear has always been up to now, just an inherent part of myself that I have always accepted. I always sleep with the landing light on"

"I think I have been having a memory of being back in the pram. I can remember feeling a thud as the crow landed on the hood, and I remember the light being blocked as the crow jumped down onto me. What I have come to realise, is that it's the bird that took away the light."

"I don't think that the crow was pecking at me, I think it was just curious. Its claws scratched me as it tried to escape. What frightened me most about that day was the noise and sensation of the flapping wings in my face, the loss of light and most of all, the terrifying sound of my mother's screams and clapping hands as she rushed towards me."

I was surprised when she revealed that she believed that it was the loss of light and her mother's extreme reaction to the crow which had triggered her anxiety and phobia, not the crow itself. As she got older it was the flapping of bird's wings or the fading of light that would trigger her ongoing anxiety and fear, as though something dreadful was about to happen, but now, understanding these things, she no longer feared the fear.

This understanding had brought her great comfort, but she had decided not to share this realisation with her mother, as she thought it would distress her too much. To find out, after all these years, that it was her screaming and reaction to the crow which had triggered her daughters phobia, would be too confronting, she would be devastated. I agreed.

We continued with the session, and I induced trance and gave positive suggestions about *being as she wanted to be*, about moving to London, about birds, about accepting change, about maintaining contact with her mother, feeling close but at a distance. I gave her a CD to use, to reinforce these suggestions and she left the session feeling very positive, looking forward to her move to London.

Sometime later her mother became my client for something unrelated.

I asked after her daughter. She smiled and reached into her handbag and pulled out a photograph.

"I brought this to show you!" She said.

It was a photo of her daughter on holiday in Venice, standing in St Mark's Square, laughing, arms outstretched in the sun, surrounded by hundreds and hundreds of pigeons!

Years later, after having emigrated to Australia I had the privilege of encountering a huge cassowary walking slowly along a road in the Daintree Rainforest. Perfectly camouflaged it had emerged from the forest like a feathered dinosaur, looking me straight in the eye, and walking alongside my car for meters, unperturbed. As I quickly wound up my window, my thoughts returned to this lady, and I wondered how she would have responded in this situation.

Footnote

Sing a Song of Sixpence is an English Nursery Rhyme possibly originating in the 18th century.

It was first published in print in Tommy Thumbs 'Pretty Song Book,' in London around 1744.

Sing a song of sixpence,
A pocket full of rye.
Four and twenty blackbirds
Baked in a pie.
When the pie was opened
The birds began to sing;
Wasn't that a dainty dish
To set before the king?

The king was in his counting house,
Counting out his money;
The queen was in the parlour,
Eating bread and honey.

The maid was in the garden,
Hanging out the clothes,
When down came a blackbird.
And pecked off her nose.

Sometimes, a fifth verse is added, to moderate the ending!

There was such commotion,
That little Jenny wren
Flew down into the garden,
And put it back again!

Many people came to me over the years looking for help with phobias, A phobia is a type of anxiety disorder and can be described as a persistent, excessive, unrealistic fear of an object, person, animal, activity, or situation.

A person with a phobia can either try to avoid the thing that triggers the fear or has to endure it as best they can, suffering great anxiety and distress. Most of the phobias I dealt with involved dogs, spiders, or birds and many were caused by unfortunate experiences or trauma that had occurred involving a negative encounter with the animal when they were children.

Bird phobias were surprisingly common. I had one client who had been chased by a flock of geese as a four-year-old who had been so affected by the trauma that he had developed a stutter. Another client who had a lifelong fear of birds (ornithophobia), was able through hypnosis to discover that this fear had been caused by the large, feathered hanging mobile which had rotated above his cot as a baby! Another woman was able to reveal after hypnotherapy that her bird phobia had been the result of the nursery wallpaper that featured colourful exotic birds with beady eyes, which had terrified her as she lay as a baby in her cot.

Uncovering and understanding the origins of their phobias which had either been repressed or had occurred when they were so young that they could not verbalise their fear, was extremely powerful. Being able to understand and rationalise the cause of the phobia as an adult and see it from an adult perspective, helped these clients to bring about positive changes so that they were able to understand and move beyond the event.

21

FOOD FOR THOUGHT

Wanting to lose weight was the request of many of the people who I saw privately. Men, women, young and old and even children brought along by their parents. At the time there were lots of articles in magazines and programmes on television suggesting hypnotherapy as a successful treatment for weight loss.

Many people found success in weight loss through attending groups, using appetite suppressants, or following strict diets, exercise regimes or even surgery.

I tended to work with the people who felt they had already tried everything else and failed miserably. With some it was a sweet tooth, with others it was junk food. Some loved cooking, some ate for comfort, while others hated exercise or were unable to exercise. They came with little hope, I was their last resort, but all felt they were not happy with themselves and their size. No two people were the same.

This lady who came to me about her weight was a friend of a friend and we had met briefly socially. When she found out that I was a hypnotherapist, she was extremely interested and asked if hypnotherapy could help her lose weight. I suggested she book in for a free consultation and I would explain then how hypnotherapy worked, and we could take it from there.

About a year later she did book in. She was beautifully dressed, wore nice jewellery, had shiny hair, and well applied makeup. She'd obviously spent a lot of time and money on the body that she didn't like.

She said she had always been a bit plump, but after her wedding and having two babies within two years, she had found it impossible to lose weight. She told me her life was very busy with the children, a large home, and a dog to look after. Her elderly parents were kind and supportive but lived many hours' drive away, so were not always able to help out.

Her husband worked away. He earned very good money – he worked offshore for two weeks at a time and then spent two weeks at home. When he was home, he had no interest in her, the children or family life. He spent as little time there as possible, preferring to be out with his mates, drinking, going to the casino or attending sports events.

Her husband recently stated that he didn't find her attractive anymore, he didn't want to be seen with her or the children, and he gave the ultimatum that if she didn't lose weight, then he wanted a divorce.

Hearing this had been devastating and left her feeling rejected and lonely She said this was not what she wanted her marriage to be, and was not even sure if she still wanted to be with her husband but was thinking of the children, the dog, their families, the house and what everyone else would think if the marriage failed. She was in tears.

She was surprised and embarrassed to have opened up about all of this, she had just come to see me to lose weight. I explained that the body had lots of basic needs, shelter, nourishment, affection, belonging and to feel nurtured – so many things. If these things were not forthcoming, if there was an emptiness or a need then sometimes, the body held on to weight, almost as if it were filling up the void inside.

I talked about hypnotherapy. I explained how it worked, what it felt like, and how it could unlock things that had been hidden in the back of her mind that were causing her to have this weight problem now. She was interested as although she wasn't sure what the future held she still wanted to lose weight for herself, her self-confidence and for her children, to be able to enjoy times with them without feeling tired or self-conscious. She didn't want to be criticised, rejected, or looked down upon just for being fat.

This conversation took up the full hour, but she was determined to book in and see me for sessions to help her. She returned the following week. Her husband was still away, and she had been feeling increasingly angry towards him and was not looking forward to his next visit home. She was keen to start with hypnosis.

I induced trance and was surprised how quickly she went into a deep trance. She became very still and pale and started talking in a very quiet polite voice using old-fashioned phrases.

I put a tape into my cassette recorder as I usually did in these situations, as it was probable that she wouldn't remember what she said in trance when she opened her eyes.

She told me her story.

It was a story from long ago. Her name was Grace, (it was not the name she used now). She told me she lived in London and gave me the address and the names of her mother, father, and siblings.

She said she wasn't unwell but was very weak because she felt unable to eat. Doctors had not been able to help. The whole family was very upset because they didn't know what to do. She told me they loved her very much.

She was speaking in a whisper now, and complained that her mouth was very dry.

"Please may I have some water?"

I got a glass of water, she sat up slowly and sipped it, the hand holding the glass trembling, then continued her story, still in trance, whispering, "I can't eat."

And you can't eat?

" I don't want to live anymore."

I acknowledged her statement… *and you don't want to live any more.*

Tears rolled silently down her cheeks.

"I have received such dreadful news. My fiancé is dead. He's never coming home."

The story unfolded.

Her fiancé had been in the military. She told me his name and date of birth, his company and rank. She was seventeen and he was twenty when they'd met at a ball in London and fallen completely in love. Their respective parents already knew one another, and the couple had spent a few wonderful months courting until their families had agreed that they could become engaged. It was decided by both families that they should wait to get married, as it was the time of the Boer War, and her fiancé was being sent with his company to South Africa. On his return, they would marry.

"We had an understanding," she said. "We were betrothed."

He departed and she was heartbroken. The only thing that made his absence bearable was the wonderful wedding she was planning at the parish church for when they would be married on his return.

Her fiancé survived the war and was on his way back home, but then his family received the dreadful news that he had died on board the ship, and his body had been buried at sea.

When Grace was told this, her world fell apart. She retreated to her room and took to her bed. She couldn't eat and would drink only water. She pined away. Within six weeks she was dead.

"My heart was broken," she said, "I could not live without him."

She went very quiet and lay still with her eyes shut.

After some time, I asked... *and what's happening now?*

She said, "I'm back here now, with you!"

She had spontaneously moved out of trance into the present.

I asked what her name was, and she gave me the name that she had come to the appointment with that day. I was very relieved!

She opened her eyes, sat up and said, "That really freaked me out!"

I nearly said I was freaked out too but stopped myself!

She said that all the time that she had been talking, she had known that she was actually in the room with me, but that she had been totally caught up in her other life – it had been vividly real.

I understood exactly what she meant, remembering back to my own first experience of being hypnotised, when I had become a child again, and sobbed over Spot the Spaniel, feeling his silky ears, and remembering how he smelt. I knew how powerful the experience must have been for her.

She asked, "Do you think... I can't lose weight... because to me, losing weight means I die?"

Before I could answer, she went on to say, "Because I think that's exactly what happened. And now I know what it feels like to be truly in love, and I can tell you, that's not what I have now, or have ever had with my husband."

We talked some more. I gave her the tape I'd recorded of the session, and I suggested that she listen to it at home. I would have liked her to have made another appointment, I was concerned that there was still more that needed to be explored, but she said she would call me soon. She was focused, energised and as she left, seemed very much in control.

I didn't hear from her again, I hoped that she was doing well, but eventually I did hear about her, from our mutual friend.

I was astonished when this friend told me that immediately after the hypnotherapy session, my client had rung her parents letting them know how unhappy she was, and the problems with her marriage and husband. They were very supportive and she'd arranged to take the children and dog and live with them until she had sorted things out. She'd packed the car, and had walked out of her marital home leaving everything else behind. Her friend was shocked, I hoped that my client would be all right.

About a year later I was approached by a stranger in town.

"You don't recognise me, do you?" she asked.

I had been caught out again!

She laughed and told me her name. It was my client. I was totally amazed, and I was not surprised I hadn't recognised her, she had been a size twenty-eight and was now a size ten. She was beautifully dressed, and radiated health and positive energy. She looked amazing, so slim and graceful, completely transformed from the unhappy, overweight woman who had originally come to see me.

She ushered me into a nearby tea shop and sat me down. We ordered and she began.

"After that session with you, I decided I had to move out, I couldn't stay with my husband any longer! So, I phoned my parents, explained my marriage was over and asked if I could come home. They agreed, and I took everything I wanted from the house, put the children and the dog in the car and left!

"My husband arrived home a week later to an empty house! I got a solicitor who dealt with everything, my husband agreed to the divorce and settlement. The house sold quickly, and I got my share. I've heard he's moved on with a new younger woman and we've had no contact since. He's got no interest in seeing me or the children, I have sole custody."

She told me that she was enrolled on a beauty therapist course, loved her new body, the children were happy and doing well in their new school, and she had a lot of support from her family.

Then she said, "I have something else to tell you."

When she had arrived at her parent's home, she had told them about what had transpired during our hypnotherapy session. Her parents had been understandably concerned and insisted on listening to the recording of the session with her. They couldn't believe it, and after hearing the recording, they were even more concerned.

Then she had told them that there was something that she felt she had to do. She needed to go to London to try to find the house that Grace had lived in previously and any other information about her past life and her soldier fiancé. She felt that she couldn't move on and needed to know for herself.

"My parents thought I had lost the plot!" She laughed. "But when they finally realised that I was determined to go, my mother agreed to look after the children and my father said that he would come with me to help. I was relieved, as I had never been to London before!"

Then she said, "Now I'm really going to freak you out!"

She told me that she and her father had found Grace's house!

She was right, I was freaked out, but more was to come.

She told me the house was there, at the exact address she had given me on the tape, but it had now been divided into apartments. She stood outside and took photographs of the exterior and knew it was the house from the moment she saw it. She remembered it.

Then, they had gone to the nearest church and looked through church records. She found the date of Grace's christening and the date of her burial. With help from the Church Warden, they eventually found Grace's gravestone. They'd tended the overgrown grave, bought flowers, placed them on the grave, and had taken photographs. She said her father had been completely bemused at first but had eventually been so supportive and became totally involved and very emotional as each piece of information from the taped session became a reality.

Then they had gone to the War Museum, to attempt to find records of her fiancé but no one could find any trace of his details or even a mention of his company.

She refused to give up and had asked where else they could look. They were advised to try a different department and were helped by an assistant, who finally discovered that her fiancés military company had been amalgamated with another. It now had a different name to the one that she had known, but it was real, it had existed, and finally, his name as she had spoken it on the tape, was found.

Of course, there was no grave, her fiancé had been buried at sea, but she and her father had placed flowers into the Thames in his memory. She told me that she cried as she watched the flowers float down the river towards the sea, but she had felt such inner peace and completeness, everything had now fallen into place for her.

I was in tears in the tea shop by now.

She took my hand and said, "You gave me back my life that day, I will never forget it."

Then she said, "But that's not the only strange thing, now I'm going to freak you out even more!"

I listened, wondering what more there could possibly be.

She went on to tell me that after being hypnotised that day, she had immediately begun to lose weight. She laughed and told me that she had not had to alter her eating in any way. She hadn't dieted, hadn't reduced portion sizes and hadn't exercised. She had simply allowed her body to become slim, and it had!

She smiled and said, "Now that I know what true love feels like, I will never settle for anything less. I am hopeful that one day I will again meet the man I am supposed to be with."

I was hopeful for her too.

"And there is nothing left remarkable
Beneath the visiting moon."

Cleopatra on the death of Mark Anthony.
Anthony and Cleopatra by William Shakespeare.

Footnote

I have known people with dramatic weight loss after dieting or gastric banding. Often there can be a problem with unsightly excess skin that is not elastic enough to recover. I have also seen dramatic weight loss in terminally ill people, they certainly do not glow with health, but I have never before witnessed such weight loss as I saw in my client. Her skin was taut and young and vibrant. She honestly looked ten years younger.

Many people over the years have asked me to "do a past life regression" with them. I understand this fascination and curiosity, but I have never accepted such a request. Part of me was uncomfortable with the whole idea of past lives. I had been taught how to manage past lives on various training courses, but had decided then, that it wasn't for me, I felt out of my comfort zone. That being said, several clients of mine had spontaneously seemed to move into what genuinely appeared to be a past life regression and I was grateful that I had the skills and knowledge to work with this reality and then be able to bring them safely back into the present.

I must say that the past life experience was always profound for the client. Many said that they had never believed in such things before, but that it was real, and they were there, then. In the context of their therapy, experiencing a past life regression was extremely powerful and dramatically helped them to understand and overcome the problem that they had originally presented with.

It was extraordinary to me, that my client after experiencing this spontaneous regression, had been able to travel to London, a place that she had never been to before, and was then able to find her house as she remembered it, her own grave and her fiancés name and regiment details.

I had another client who under hypnosis started speaking in a language I did not recognise. She apparently understood perfectly what I said to her in English, but she could not respond to my questions in English, despite having walked into the session speaking perfect English!

In exasperation she attempted to communicate with me during the session by taking my notepad and pen and making a series of marks on the paper which she expected me to be able to read, but which I could still not understand.

Subsequently in frustration, looking for answers she had taken the recorded tape of her session and the paper on which she had drawn, to a university, where the 'writing' was eventually recognised and found to be a 'dead' ancient Middle Eastern Language. Neither she nor her family had ever had any connection with that part of the world. I later heard from her that she had begun working with the language expert at the university, using self-hypnosis to induce trance, in order to help him to translate ancient texts!

One of the strangest experiences I had was with a client who had moved further and further back in time giving dates, names, village names and speaking in different regional accents. At various times throughout sessions, she became in turn a man with a deep man's voice, a woman, and then a young child with a child's voice. I wasn't sure where we were going with all these past lives, when she suddenly stopped talking altogether and did not respond to any of my questions, and lay completely still in the chair, eyes closed. Thankful of my training, I knew how to bring her out of this non-responsive state. When she was back and fully herself again, I asked her what had been happening, when she had been unable to speak to me.

She looked at me with exasperation and said, "Of course I couldn't talk… I was a tree!"

This experience altered forever my attitude towards pruning trees in the garden!

Some therapists can become very involved when working with such cases, exploring the past life experiences of clients over a long period of time, taking them through many different lives and experiences.

My interest was not in exploring my client's past lives for their own fascination or historical interest, or for my own curiosity. My role as I saw it, was to help the client facilitate positive change in a way that was efficacious, held meaning for the client and would allow them to understand and address whatever it was that they had presented with for therapy.

It was because of these clients who, during the course of what I thought would be a routine hypnotherapy session, spontaneously entering into past life regressions relating events and incidents with complete conviction, that I decided I needed to know more. Their experiences were so believable and related with such certainty and brought about such dramatic life changing outcomes, that I booked myself in with a therapist who specialised in past life regressions. I explained my position – I wanted to find out more, so that if or when my clients spontaneously regressed in such a way, into a past life, then I could be better prepared to understand and help them.

The therapist explained to me that the best way to understand regression, was to experience the phenomenon for myself. So that's how it happened, as I sat back in his reclining chair, he took me back into my own past life.

The story of my past life regression will have to be told another time.

I still have the tape recording made of the session; it is very precious to me, and the experience was profound. Listening back to the voice that was mine yet not mine, I gained important and valuable insight into my own self. The experience brought me clarity and understanding as to why I had become a therapist and how and why I was able to do the therapeutic work that I did.

22

STARVED OF AFFECTION – HUNGRY FOR LOVE

I opened the door to loud knocking, to discover to my surprise, an ambulance man on the doorstep. He explained that he had brought a patient through to see me but unfortunately, he didn't think the patient would fit through the door.

My secretary had informed me that my next client that day was a man who wanted to see me about his weight, I saw many people regarding weight loss, but I had never had an issue with the size of my door before!

"Where's my client now?" I asked with concern.

"He's in the ambulance in the carpark." The ambulance man replied.

This client's appointment was scheduled to last an hour, but I knew I had a cancellation after him. I had been going to use the time to catch up on some paperwork but decided that it would give me the opportunity to leave the practice and see my client in the ambulance instead. I told my secretary what I was doing and picked up my pen and note pad and followed the ambulanceman back to the carpark. I think he was relieved that they did not have to attempt to transport his passenger up the tiny, cobbled lane to my premises.

The ambulance driver was waiting with my client and helped me into the ambulance through the side door. It was then that I realised the enormity of the situation. My client was uncomfortably occupying a large section of the ambulance, sitting in a wheelchair the size of a two-seater sofa, and he filled it.

I introduced myself, leant forward and we shook hands, and I asked if I could sit down. I then asked the two ambulance men if it would be possible to be left alone with my client so that we could talk privately. They looked at each other, nodded and gave me a thumbs up. They took flasks and newspapers and retreated to a nearby bench.

I hardly needed to ask my client what the problem was, but I did ask how he wanted me to help.

He said, "I think you can help me because I read an article about you in the local paper. It said that you look for the cause of the problem. I know I've got a problem, I'm not stupid, I know that my eating is killing me, but I still cannot control my eating. If I knew the cause then maybe I can stop."

"I have been overweight my entire life," he continued. "As a child my mother would put me on diets, but I had such a need to eat that I would go to the shed and take potatoes straight from the sack, brush off the soil and eat them raw. That's how much I needed to eat. I couldn't sleep unless I felt full."

"I've seen health professionals and dieticians and now I attend a clinic at the hospital, but nothing makes a difference. I just get larger and larger, and I don't want to live like this, and I don't want to die."

I asked how he managed day to day.

It seemed that all his physical needs were met. His home was cleaned, meals prepared, and he had a team of people using hoists to attend to his personal requirements. Some carers were really kind, but some were horrid. He felt that some found him disgusting and repulsive, and made him feel ashamed and embarrassed, but there was one older lady who was wonderful. He told me she spoke to him kindly, and sometimes sang as she washed him gently, massaged him with creams and carefully applied medicated powder to all the folds of his skin. She made him feel human and cherished and he looked forward to the days that she came. He also had a little dog called Scamp for company.

"What do you do to occupy yourself?" I asked.

"I watch my favourite videos; I like cartoons and Disney movies. I don't watch much TV as I can't change the channels if something frightening comes on. My mother comes to visit on weekends."

"Does anything affect your eating?" I asked. "Do you have good days and bad days"

"Every day is a bad day." He replied. "But the nights are worse."

"I get frantic if my fridge and pantry aren't full. I have to know that I have crisps and cakes and biscuits and puddings available. Night is the worst because I hate to be alone in the dark, I keep the lights on all night. The worst time, day or night is if there is a storm. When there's thunder and lightning, I just stuff anything into my mouth, I have to eat."

I was intrigued to know how he managed to obtain all this food; his size meant that he would not be mobile.

"I keep food I can reach easily in my locker, next to my bed," he replied.

It seemed that the lady next door was very kind and helped by doing all his grocery shopping and she also refilled his cupboards and locker. He paid her son to walk his little dog Scamp mornings and evenings.

He looked embarrassed. "And I also pay him to bring me extra food. Each evening he brings me meals, family size fish and chips or Chinese or Indian takeaway or burgers. I get him to remove all the evidence, the containers, and bags so that my carers don't see them the next morning. I'm supposed to be on a calorie-controlled diet."

But now he had a problem, this arrangement was going to end soon, because the neighbours' son was moving away and joining the army. My client was becoming quite anxious and didn't know what he was going to do. He was absolutely ashamed of his overeating, but only when he felt completely full, was he able to sleep.

"The other day when there was a storm," he said, "The lights went out. I always keep a torch near me, I hate the dark and I grabbed tins from the locker opened them and started eating, because that is what I always do. It wasn't until the lights came back on, that I realised that I was eating Scamp's dog food!" He started sobbing, his whole body shook, "I can't go on living like this, every day is awful."

He was thirsty after all this talking; I handed him his bottle of water. I asked him if he wanted to be hypnotised, to find out the cause of the problem. He readily agreed. I went to the door and spoke to the ambulance men outside and told them that I needed about another hour with my client, would that be all right?

Thumbs up again.

I was amazed at how quickly he accepted my suggestions and went deep into trance.

... And drifting back in time... to the cause of this problem.
... Or something related to the cause of this problem...

He immediately began shivering and shaking. His arms were jerking about and then he made the most dreadful wailing sound that sounded like pain, despair, or hopelessness – whatever he was reliving – it was ghastly.

I kept with him in the moment, acknowledging each shudder or cry. I tried to move time on, and I believe I did, but it continued as more of the same. Whatever it was that he was experiencing, it was prolonged.

The noise he was making must have caused alarm outside, because I saw the ambulance drivers face appear at the door looking in anxiously. I gave him a thumbs up and waved him away.

When the episode had continued for about ten minutes, and I had been unable to move time on, I finally said.

... And after all of this
and when it's not like this anymore,
and you don't shiver and shake,
and you don't cry out
and you are safe at last
and all that lets you know that you are safe at last
and then the difference that you know
about food, and eating, and size, and weight,
and how you feel about yourself,
and caring enough about yourself,
to care enough about yourself.
... And how that feels.

The shivering and crying stopped, and to my surprise his hands went to up his face and his neck, and he touched his arms and body and he smiled. I think what he was visualising and touching, and what I was seeing was very different indeed.

And as this now begins,

and taking all the time that you need
for your body to know how to do this
in a way that is safe
so that there really can be those changes
and all the difference this difference makes
to you, and to Scamp and to your mother…
He was really smiling now.
… And you will remember as much of this as you need to remember
… and you will forget as much as you need to forget.
Then and only then,
your eyes will open into the here and now…
Safe here in the ambulance with Gail.

After some time, he opened his eyes and complained that he was really cold. There was a blanket nearby, so I covered him up and held his hand. I didn't speak. I wanted to hear what he had to say.

"I heard everything," he said. "And I wanted to talk, and tell you what was happening but couldn't, I felt so small, I felt… that I hadn't learnt to talk yet."

I nodded my understanding of his preverbal state.

"I think I know what that was all about." He said. "When I was a teenager my mum told me about the first few days of my life. I wasn't that interested then and I never made the connection before today, but now I do."

"My mum was extremely poor and lived in a rented room in a house near the docks. It was war time and she worked nights in a munitions factory. She had not known she was pregnant until the day she gave birth to me, alone in her room. She didn't know what to do, so wrapped me in a towel and put me into a drawer under the bed. Desperate to keep her job, she arranged with a neighbour who had also recently had a baby to come to the room that evening. This neighbour would spend the night with the two babies, feeding them both so that my mother could continue going to work. The neighbour was paid for her services."

"So, the same day I was born, my mother caught the bus for the night shift and went to work as usual, leaving me in the care of the neighbour. This arrangement worked well until the fifth night."

"On this night the neighbour had still not arrived by the time my mother had to catch the bus, but she left anyway, leaving her room unlocked, thinking that the neighbour would arrive within minutes. Unfortunately, there was an air raid, and the neighbour was instructed to go directly to the nearest air raid shelter. This neighbour was not concerned as she believed that my mother would still be with me and that we would both have gone together to an air raid shelter too. She didn't know that my mother had already left for work."

Bombs were dropped all night. The area around the docks was targeted and the devastation was widespread. There were explosions, fires, rescue teams, sirens, and ambulances all around.

"I was alone, all night," he said.

The five-day old baby left alone in the drawer had learnt hunger, fear, cold, wet, and dirty. He had been terrified by the explosions and sirens and was covered in debris when the windows had blown in. He had screamed and screamed lying hungry, wet, cold, and frightened in the dark until he had no voice left, but still no one had come.

His mother had returned at the end of her shift to find the area flattened and on fire. She tried to get through but was held back and was told it wasn't safe. She screamed that her baby was still in the house but was assured that the rescue services had already been through all the houses and not found or heard a baby, but she wouldn't give up. Eventually they allowed her through and accompanied her into the house. The front door was blown in and there was no glass left in any of the windows, but thankfully the building had not caught fire and the staircase was still intact. They ran upstairs to her room, and she reached under the bed and pulled out the drawer. Her baby was lying there, completely still. His eyes were wide open, and he wasn't even crying. His mother had told him years later, that he hadn't been affected by what had happened and "must have slept through the whole thing."

But his body had remembered the trauma of the experience. His body knew about hunger, and cold, and being alone, about explosions and flashing lights and his body knew that he needed food, comfort and saving.

Then my client said something that astounded me.

He said, "I think I am still that baby. I still need to be fed and cleaned, I still need people to help me move and to look after me. I have never had a father but I'm going to have to learn to be a father now to the baby part of me who needs to know he can grow up. I understand now why I don't like storms and lightning and the dark – it's like being back with the bombs, and I understand now why I have to eat."

Once he had expressed this thought, it was as though a switch had flipped. He was energised and keen to get back home. He thanked me and asked me to call the ambulance men over to take him back. Before they left, I told him that if he needed to talk again we could do so over the phone. He thanked me again but said that he thought that this would not be necessary! I felt superfluous to requirement – he didn't need me anymore!

I never heard from him again, but I did hear about him.

A year later, I accepted onto my training course, a nurse who told me at interview that she had witnessed first-hand the healing power of hypnosis. She worked in a local hospital obesity clinic and knew a man there who told her that he had been to see me for hypnotherapy. I knew exactly who it was, and I asked how he was doing.

"He is the most successful patient we have ever had." She said. "He is an inspiration to our other patients and gives them hope. He has already lost nearly half his body weight and goes for long walks everyday with his little dog."

I knew that getting through doors would no longer be a problem. Doors would now be open to him.

23

GIVING TALKS – MEMORABLE FOR THE WRONG REASONS!

Right from the beginning of my career, I was happy to go and give talks to groups of people about my work. This was especially important when I first started in order to gain new clients.

These groups were varied. I spoke to small groups of women who were more interested in the supper they were going to be eating afterwards than in what any speaker had to say. I spoke to professional groups and medical experts, which was always nerve-wracking. I did after-dinner speeches, and I spoke to Rotary and Lions, Women's Institutes and Young Farmers. I went to all kinds of establishments, and I adjusted each talk to the audience I found myself facing

I didn't have a fixed fee, I often charged nothing, and my only payment would be a strong cup of tea and a delicious fresh baked scone. If I was lucky then "leftovers" wrapped in serviettes would be pushed into my hands on the way out, "for later." Some groups would only cover my travel expenses, while others were very generous and I would receive remuneration in a card in an envelope with a basket of flowers and chocolates presented at the close, with photographs taken that would appear in the local paper the following week.

I was not too worried about payment, as I always received many enquiries following one of my talks, which would lead to initial free consultations, then paid appointments later. I usually did a demonstration on someone from the audience and that always went down very well and would again result in people booking in at a later date. I would also distribute leaflets with my details, and explanations of some of the problems I could help with, such as smoking, anxiety, phobias, or weight.

Certainly, at the beginning, giving talks was a really good way of generating interest and appointments. I used to get lots of new private clients following a talk. However, some talks were unfortunately memorable for all the wrong reasons.

After work one day I went to a local hotel, where a professional group of women met once a month and had a speaker after dinner. I was duly introduced to the ladies, about twenty of them. They had positioned themselves on chairs in a circle, so I joined in. Some were very excited, some looked nervous, some of the ladies there were previous clients, but I did not acknowledge them, preserving their confidentiality. Other ladies looked quite hostile, they didn't believe in "such things" they said, they weren't going to be duped. Some said they were good Christians, and they weren't sure if it was okay, was it the Devil's work?

I reassured them that I only had good intentions for my clients and explained that many of my clients were referred to me by medical practitioners and that a retired nurse and vicar's wife also worked with me. This seemed to placate them, Doctors, nurses and vicar's wives being respectable and well-educated.

I explained how I had decided to train as a hypnotherapist, following my career as a teacher. The ladies became engaged, and I gave some case histories, giving no names and changing a few details to ensure confidentiality, which was always paramount, particularly in these small-town communities where everyone knew everyone.

Then I did a suggestibility test.

I got the ladies to focus on their clasped hands with the index fingers sticking straight out. As I talked, I suggested that their fingers would begin to move together.

Gasp... they did!

Then I got their fingers to "stick" together.

Gasp... they did!

Then I got their fingers to "unstick" and open.

Most did come unstuck, some didn't – it just took them a bit longer. They had to concentrate on their own fingers, not look over at what the other ladies were doing.

I explained that the fingers would want to pull together naturally, the interesting part to me was when they opened. This indicated that the person was open to my suggestions.

I explained that anyone could be hypnotised if they wanted to be, and no one would be hypnotised if they didn't want to be. I told them people with a high IQ made good subjects. I asked if anyone would like to be hypnotised in front of the group. To my complete amazement, they all wanted to be hypnotised, even the original sceptics.

So, I decided to do them all together.

Big mistake! I had never done this many people together before.

I lowered my voice, and used calm, monotonous, repetitious words. Slowly, one by one the eyes around the room closed. All of them. I then went round the room. I put this lady's hand up in the air saying it was held up by rope. For another I made a leg heavy, or a leg light, so it was sticking up above the ground. To another lady I tied imaginary helium balloons to her wrist, so her arm bobbed and floated in the air, another I stuck to the chair that she was sitting on.

Round the circle I went, describing something different with a limb or body of each lady. I began to feel like a stage hypnotist.

Then I got them to test the suggestions.

Arms stayed up even though they tugged. Legs wouldn't move even though they heaved, those I had stuck to chairs were unable to get up. There were mumblings and worried noises – they couldn't believe what was happening to them.

I told them to keep their eyes closed while I went back around the circle and touched each person gently on the shoulder. As I touched their shoulders, I told them that all normal feelings and functions would return.

Slowly eyes opened, there were gasps of astonishment, surprise and much talking amongst themselves. Then, to my horror, I noticed one lady still slumped over, crying in her chair. I went over and touched her shoulder again. Everyone was watching, she was still crying out, bent over and holding her knee, sobbing, "my leg, my leg."

Her friend sitting beside her told me that some years earlier this lady had been in a dreadful road accident, in which her leg had been horribly crushed. She'd spent a long time being treated in hospital, and had to be taught how to walk again. I was grateful that her friend was there to tell me this because now I knew I could move time on, until after the accident, after the pain, and after the recovery until she could once again do all those things she could do now.

This I did, telling her in front of everyone, that when she felt fully recovered, and able to do all that she was able to do when she came into this room that evening, then and only then, her eyes would open. I told her she only needed to remember what she wanted to remember, about what had just happened, or she could choose not to remember.

We waited.

There was complete silence in the room as all the ladies watched. She finally, very calmly opened her eyes. She said it had been an amazing experience. She said she had felt the fear and the pain just as she had immediately after the accident, but she felt fine now.

Everyone was gathered around, concerned for her, and relieved at the outcome. I explained to them that we can say "we put things out of our minds", or at the "back of our minds", but that these things are always there and can be remembered and retrieved. I was very fortunate that day, the lady was very forgiving, and she said she felt fine.

This experience brought about interesting questions from the other ladies present. One lady said she had been badly bitten by a huge dog when she was a child and was now terrified of all dogs. Could hypnotherapy help her? She later came to me as a client and had successful treatment. She now owns a large dog.

I never did a group demonstration again. There are just too many unknowns, I had been fortunate that the lady's friend had been there to let me know about the car accident.

I prepared to leave, it had been quite an involved and stressful evening and I still had an hour to drive home. As I was getting into my car, I was called back urgently by the hotel manager. He asked me to come back inside.

It turned out that one of his staff had gone missing, having delivered drinks to our group earlier that evening. The waiter had just been found, standing behind a curtain in the room in which I had been addressing the ladies. The waiter had been interested in what I was going to say and had crept back in to listen to the talk. He had been there for the suggestibility test when I had stuck the ladies' fingers together, but his fingers had failed to come apart afterwards! He had been standing there terrified, with his fingers stuck together the whole evening, not knowing what to do.

I unstuck him – he was extremely embarrassed and nearly in tears. He had been so frightened. He knew he shouldn't have gone behind the curtain, but he had wanted to listen to the hypnotherapist talk.

I recognised him when he booked in as a client some months later. He was a very good hypnotic subject and got from the session what he wanted.

I became more cautious with my talks and demonstrations. You never know what experiences people have been through that could be triggered under hypnosis, or who might be listening.

Another evening, another talk.

This time the venue was an hour away from work, but in a different direction. I hadn't been there before.

I had been asked to talk to a group of older ladies. They had a reputation for providing a very good supper, and I was not to be disappointed.

The food was already laid out when I got there, trestle tables groaning with plates of wonderful homemade baking. Busy ladies with aprons, bustling about with coffee, cups of tea, sausage rolls, homemade pies and sandwiches, scones, fruit loaves and lively conversation. I joined in gladly.

After everything had been consumed and cleared away, I was formally introduced.

As I stood up and started to speak, the hysterical laughter started.

Three ladies in the front row were bent double in their seats, laughing, crying, and clutching each other. I could barely open my mouth without them setting off again. There were a lot of stern looks, shushing and tut-tutting going on from behind them, but nothing was going to stop their enjoyment. I wondered if the cakes had been spiked!

I talked about how I got into hypnotherapy; it was a nightmare. Even when I was being serious, my words were met with hysterical laughter. They were unstoppable. By now tissues had come out and they were howling uncontrollably. I made the sensible decision not to do a demonstration. I gave a few case histories and I tried to answer questions. As I prepared to leave after a very challenging hour, the three ladies approached me, still clutching each other, helpless with laughter.

It wasn't just me looking confused, the Chairperson had already come over to me and apologised profusely for their behaviour.

The three ladies thanked me for coming such a long way. I smiled. Then to my astonishment, they pulled out autograph books from their handbags.

Perplexed, I asked, "What would you like me to write?"

"Your name," they spluttered.

"And what would that be?" I asked.

They were beside themselves with laughter.

"Pam Ayres of course!"

I was getting more confused by the minute. Pam Ayres is an English poet, comedian, song writer and at the time was appearing on many radio and TV programmes. She wrote and read hilarious poems, in her distinctive accent, one of which, "Oh I wish I'd looked after me Teeth," was voted in the top ten of the Nation's favourite poems!

I did not look like Pam Ayres, I did not speak like Pam Ayres, and I did not think that anything I had said that night had been remotely funny, yet these three ladies were utterly convinced that that is who I was.

I took their books and pens, and I wrote in each with a smile, "Greetings from Pam Ayres," signing her name with a flourish!

They were quite overcome and followed me outside to my car, thanking me profusely and waving me off. I waved back.

I felt terrible all the way home. I still feel terrible about my duplicity all these years later. My sincere apologies to Pam Ayres. I was always told that to be a good therapist, one had to put one foot in the client's reality but keep one foot firmly in one's own. On that occasion, I absolutely crossed the line.

I do hope those ladies never found out that they were duped. If Pam Ayres ever finds out, again, I apologise. I was in a very awkward position, and those ladies were utterly convinced I was Pam Ayers, I couldn't disappoint them.

But Pam can rest assured that her reputation remains intact. It is my understanding that following an excellent supper she delivered an evening of entertaining stories received with hilarious laughter bringing happy memories to three old ladies!

I was getting a bit tired of giving talks. I was working full-time in Psychology now and had more clients than I could cope with. I was beginning to feel old and worn out. This talk, I had decided, was to be my last.

Again, it was a long drive, the last part being over wide-open fells on a dusty one-track road to a very isolated village. It was a lovely autumn afternoon and I put the roof down on my new car.

I hadn't realised that today was the day I was giving a talk until I got to work and looked in my diary. I usually made a bit of an effort if I was giving a talk, and I felt a bit underdressed. So, at lunchtime, I dashed out to the shops and quickly bought a new dress and shoes. I got back to work just in time for my next client, I was hungry, having not had time for lunch but I looked considerably smarter.

After work, I set off for the talk, by now I was extremely hungry. I was hoping for a nice cup of tea and a scone when I got there. It was a long drive, but I arrived on time and went inside. It was all very formal – I think there had been an Annual General Meeting. There was a top table with flowers and tablecloth, and it was very well attended by smartly dressed people. There was no scone, no cup of tea, just a glass of lukewarm water.

I was introduced, they clapped politely and off I went with my talk. I gave lots of information, lots of case histories, and lots of explanations, followed by answering lots of questions from the floor. They wanted me to go on and on, but I had done my allocated time and more. I was hungry, and tired, had a two-hour drive home, and it was going to get dark soon. I was not looking forward to the long-isolated drive back.

I went to the ladies' room before I left. The secretary followed me in and thanked me for my 'rather interesting talk.' She then pressed into my hand 'something for my expenses'. It was a single coin – I felt underwhelmed. I mentally calculated the cost of my new dress, my new shoes, the petrol, and the wear and tear on my new car from the single-track, dusty road.

I politely asked her if the group had a favourite charity, "Yes, we do," she replied.

I handed her back the coin and asked her to donate it. She was overwhelmed and thanked me profusely.

I escaped with the roof down and music playing. No more talks, I vowed.

As I got onto the single-track road, I needed all my wits about me. I watched for bumps and potholes. There was a beautiful sunset. All was going well until I noticed a white blob at the side of the road further down the track. I hadn't seen a single vehicle on my way out and so far, none on my way back. I slowed down, I even turned down the music. There by the side of the road was a large woolly sheep looking extremely depressed. There wasn't another sheep in sight. As I approached slowly, taking care not to startle the animal, it looked straight at me and made one almighty leap and committed suicide under the front of my car.

I stopped and got out. The sheep was no longer depressed, it was dead. My new car was stuck there on the single-track road with a huge dead sheep wedged firmly underneath it. My beautiful new car had an enormous dent in the front and side, and bits were hanging off. I cried. Not for the sheep I confess, but for me and my beautiful car.

I stood there in my new dress and new heels and grabbed handfuls of greasy wool and tried to pull the sheep out. It was stuck. I was now covered in dust; my new shoes were ruined, and I smelt of dead sheep. I was dreading that the next car along would be the ladies from the talk I had just given. I was not looking very professional, and my car was blocking the narrow road.

I heard an engine approaching from the opposite direction and an ancient Land Rover came around the corner and braked when it saw my car.

Two young farmers came over and took note of the situation, the crying lady, the dead sheep under the car and the blocked road. I thought they were going to be angry at me for killing their sheep, but they were amazing. They lifted the car and pulled the sheep out and put it in the back of their Land Rover. They checked my car over and said it was driveable, then they reversed up, until I could get past them and waved me on my way. They were so kind. It was nearly dark by this time and I set off cautiously.

I got onto the main road. Tarmac, I had reached civilization. No more sheep!

As I drove along, I spotted a pub. I pulled in. I was so hungry. Breakfast had been a long time ago, and I had missed lunch. I parked, walked in and sat down. I was given the menu.

It didn't take me long to decide.

I ordered the lamb – I felt it was poetic justice.

As I ate, I promised myself, no more talks!

AFTERWORD

When reading the chapters of this book, it may seem that these extraordinary outcomes for my clients happened in just one session. It most certainly was not always like that, but often it was.

I always started my interventions with the words, "What would you like to have happen?" This led to a positive or negative response from the client, either "I want to stop…" or "I want to be able to…" I was aware that I didn't have any answers, however, I also knew that using the right questions was vital and could often start clients on their journey of recovery.

How amazing to know that it makes perfect sense to scream with seagulls when no one else understands.

How transforming that building the train set you never had as a child can lift your dark depression and bring light inside.

How hard to comprehend that your mind can disable your hand to prevent you from strangling your own mother.

And how extraordinary to be able to give your warts to a toad that needs them, in order to make your own warts disappear, or to be able to blister your lips with an unlit cigarette.

I just needed to always remember that the presenting symptoms were the solutions waiting to happen.

In my work, I made use of Clean Language, learnt from David Grove, and I always tried to remember that I was only as good as my next question. I used words that were easily understood, and I changed the tone, speed, and volume of my voice. I was also always mindful of being age appropriate with language. I matched my breathing to the client and was aware of the importance of respecting any silence, as silence was the space between words in which meaningful change could occur.

The wise hypnotherapist also knows when it's not appropriate to work with a client using hypnosis. I was fortunate enough working within the National Health Service to be able to refer clients for whom hypnosis would not have been suitable, to other clinicians or specialists to receive treatment that would be more beneficial.

I postponed my retirement because I'd been working with a client who I believed needed my ongoing support at the end of her therapy, as she had allowed me to contact the police concerning her childhood sexual abuse.

As therapists, we were required to write up every session in a client's case file. Following my second session with this lady, after I realised the severity of what she was telling me, I felt it was probable that she could end up taking the perpetrators to court.

On the advice of my Head of Department, I chose to write, "I will never use hypnosis with this client. I believe this client may end up in Court and I do not wish to jeopardise the validity of her case."

Thank goodness I did.

Once the police became involved, all my notes from the sessions had to be handed over to the Justice System. I was told that I had to be prepared to answer questions in Court. I was forbidden from attending Court or contacting my client in any way. This was very difficult as this was the time when she most needed my support and I felt as though I was abandoning her. Her case very probably would never even have reached Court if it had been thought that I had used hypnosis with her. The Judicial System seems to think hypnotherapists plant false memories into clients – for whatever reason I can't imagine.

My client was listened to, believed, and treated with compassion by the officer from the Child Protection Unit. Her perpetrators were eventually arrested and tried. They are now serving the maximum prison sentence they could receive.

When she first shared her story with me, I'd been so shocked I cried. She apologised for making me cry. I told her that anyone hearing what she had endured should be as upset as I was because what she endured and survived was truly awful.

She later told me it was because I had cried that she decided to trust me with her whole story. The officer who interviewed her from the Child Protection Unit was also deeply moved by her story, and I was told there wasn't a dry eye in Court when she gave her evidence.

It was soon after this that a new Head of Service came to visit the Psychology Department. As I was sitting in my office, he was being shown around. He passed outside my room in the corridor, and I overheard him say to my manager, "I've heard that you have employed a hypnotist. Please tell me it's not true?"

I listened as my manager replied, "Gail is a Senior Therapist who uses hypnotherapy to obtain remarkable results, she's greatly valued by colleagues and clients, and we are fortunate to have her as part of the team."

I appreciated her support and words.

He tutted and kept on walking.

I wondered if this very senior man would ever have known how to talk to the man who screamed with seagulls.

My time was done. I was ready now to retire, to emigrate to Australia, to live out the remainder of my life with my family in the sun.

On my last day at work, I brought in a large sack of yellow daffodil bulbs. I knelt on the ground and began planting them on the grassy approach to the building. I was joined and helped by many from other departments and by the administration staff. I appreciated their help.

Every Spring, I hear from Jude in Administration when the daffodils bloom. Each year there are more flowers. There are only a few people left now, still working in that building, who would remember the hypnotherapist. Few that use the path each Spring will know who planted the daffodils, but it is enough that I know the daffodils are there and that they grow and flourish.

It is also enough for me to know that I was able to make a difference, and for all the difference that difference still makes.

'The lotus flower blooms most beautifully
from the deepest and thickest mud.'

Buddhist Proverb.

Acknowledgements

To my sister and her husband Dr Basu Chaudhuri – Val, you have always been there for me and our families in Australia, America, South Africa and the UK sharing your love and magic with us all.

To my children Anna and Roger whose teenage years were spent seeing very little of their mother who was immersed in hypnotherapy, my love, and thanks. 'The Man who Screamed with Seagulls' would still be handwritten in exercise books in a drawer somewhere, had Anna not undertaken to type my book. Thank you – these words are just not enough to express how grateful I am.

To Ernest Rossi and David Grove who taught me so much and were generous with their time and expertise, your encouragement then meant everything to me, and I will always be grateful.

To Norman Vaughton, mentor, friend, and true gentleman, my heartfelt thanks for the invaluable knowledge you shared, your insight, and your belief in me.

To Clare Jefferson a brilliant clinician and Team Lead, I have watched your career go from strength to strength over the years and know that countless people's lives have been changed for the better because of your care and expertise. A true friend, I am so glad you are in my life.

To Dr Andrew Gill and Jean Hodgkinson who worked alongside me in my private practice, thank you for bringing your professionalism and your dedication to the clients, your support was much appreciated.

To Diane Sullivan who welcomed and helped me so much as I joined the Drug and Alcohol Department of the National Health Service… a very special friend who is sadly missed.

To the managers who took a gamble on employing a hypnotherapist within the NHS system and supported me throughout my time there – I am so incredibly grateful.

To Anna Chapman and Nimmy Karat, my colleagues in psychology, you both kept me grounded and I will always remember your kindness, compassion, understanding friendship and the many much-needed mugs of tea.

To Jude Royle, Admin and Performance Manager, you deserve a medal for your kindness and efficiency in keeping me up to date with all my paperwork and the dreaded computer entries, you are such a valued friend.

To Dr Najwa Mohammed who heals bodies, minds, and spirits. Thank you for all your kindness, understanding and expert care over the years.

To Allan Soriano, Physiotherapist and Acupuncturist a true healer who not only listens but really hears.

To Dr Rebecca Dunne who encouraged me to start this book and fell down all the internet rabbit holes so that I did not have to – many thanks!

To my Australian friends, who came to my first ever book reading, bringing delicious scones and cakes, especially Joy, Kay, Neville and Max, Jenny, Chris and the lovely Gemma, Margaret, Andy, and Ted. My heartfelt thanks for your valued friendship over the years.

To Ruth Cleland, who read this book first – your valued opinion meant so much, thank you!

To the many clients who were brave enough to share your therapy journey, it has been a privilege to work with you. Without you, this book would not have been possible.

Thank you.